Leading Student-Centered Coaching

*This book is dedicated to the principal and coach teams
who work tirelessly each day in service of learning.*

Leading Student-Centered Coaching

Building Principal and Coach Partnerships

Diane Sweeney

Ann Mausbach

CORWIN
A SAGE Publishing Company

A SAGE Publishing Company

FOR INFORMATION:

Corwin

A SAGE Company

2455 Teller Road

Thousand Oaks, California 91320

(800) 233-9936

www.corwin.com

SAGE Publications Ltd.

1 Oliver's Yard

55 City Road

London EC1Y 1SP

United Kingdom

SAGE Publications India Pvt. Ltd.

B 1/I 1 Mohan Cooperative Industrial Area

Mathura Road, New Delhi 110 044

India

SAGE Publications Asia-Pacific Pte. Ltd.

3 Church Street

#10-04 Samsung Hub

Singapore 049483

Executive Editor: Dan Alpert

Associate Editor: Lucas Schleicher

Editorial Assistant: Mia Rodriguez

Production Editor: Andrew Olson

Copy Editor: Deanna Noga

Typesetter: C&M Digitals (P) Ltd.

Proofreader: Dennis W. Webb

Indexer: Judy Hunt

Cover Designer: Anupama Krishnan

Printed in the United States of America

Library of Congress Cataloging-in-Publication Data

Names: Sweeney, Diane, author. | Mausbach, Ann T., author.

Title: Leading student-centered coaching / Diane R. Sweeney and Ann Mausbach.

Description: Thousand Oaks, California : Corwin, a SAGE Company, [2018] | Includes bibliographical references.

Identifiers: LCCN 2018008232 | ISBN 9781544320557 (pbk. : alk. paper)

Subjects: LCSH: Mentoring in education. | Teachers—Training of. | School improvement programs.

Classification: LCC LB1731.4 .S867 2018 | DDC 370.102—dc23

LC record available at https://lccn.loc.gov/2018008232

This book is printed on acid-free paper.

18 19 20 21 22 10 9 8 7 6 5 4 3 2 1

Contents

Acknowledgments

There is nothing more powerful than a dedicated school leader. These leaders guide their school toward serving every student. They do this while also nurturing each staff member to grow and develop. We have been fortunate to work with, and learn from, many such leaders. We couldn't have written this without them. They live in the pages of this book.

While there are too many to name, we'd like to acknowledge and thank Kim Kazmierczak, Garry Milbourn, Mark Schuldt, Amy Glime, and Greg James. These principals have informed the practices that we shared in this book. We work with many dedicated coaches as well. The team from Nido de Aguilas in Santiago, Chile, informed our work on creating powerful principal coach partnerships. Their work is also reflected in this story.

Just as it takes a village to raise a child, it takes an amazing team to write a book. We have been fortunate to work with Dan Alpert and the Corwin staff who continually provide guidance and support. We also benefited from feedback from our critical friends at Diane Sweeney Consulting: Leanna Harris, Karen Taylor, and Julie Wright. They provided direction and clarity throughout the writing process.

While it couldn't go without saying, we can't omit a thanks to the people in our lives who motivate and inspire us the most: our husbands and children. Thanks to Dan, Quinn, Eva, Tim, Jack, and Mark. Your support and presence in our lives gives our work meaning.

PUBLISHER'S ACKNOWLEDGMENTS

Corwin gratefully acknowledges the contributions of the following reviewers:

Amanda Brueggeman
Literary Coach
Wentzville School District
Wentzville, MO

About the Authors

Diane Sweeney is the author of *Student-Centered Coaching: The Moves* (Corwin, 2016), *Student-Centered Coaching: A Guide for K–8 Coaches and Principals* (Corwin, 2011) and *Student-Centered Coaching at the Secondary Level* (Corwin, 2013). Each of these books is grounded in the simple but powerful premise that coaching can be designed to more directly impact student learning. Her first book, *Learning Along the Way* (Stenhouse, 2003), shares the story of how an urban elementary school transformed itself to become a learning community.

Diane spends her time speaking and consulting for schools and educational organizations across the country. She is also an instructor for the University of Wisconsin, Madison. When she isn't working in schools, she loves to spend time outside with her family in Denver, Colorado.

Ann Mausbach is the author of *School Leadership through the Seasons: A Guide to Staying Focused and Getting Results All Year* (Routledge Eye on Education, 2016) and *Align the Design: A Blueprint for School Improvement* (ASCD, 2008). These books provide practical guidance to school leaders interested in creating lasting reform in their schools.

Ann has served as a central office leader in a variety of roles including Coordinator of Staff Development, Director of Curriculum, Director of

Elementary Education, and Assistant Superintendent for Curriculum and Instruction. She holds a PhD from the University of Kansas. She currently works as an Assistant Professor for Educational Leadership at Creighton University in Omaha, NE.

Introduction

"Every doorway, every intersection has a story."

—Katherine Dunn

HOW WE CAME TO THIS WORK

As an instructional coach for over 20 years, Diane has spent her career helping coaches develop their skills. Ann has spent over 20 years supporting principals in their work to improve schools. Their paths crossed when Ann hired Diane to support the coaches in her district. This began a collaboration that helped them both open the door wider to understanding how critical it is to be intentional about the intersection between the principal and coach.

Both realized that they had approached the work from a distinct lens. Diane's had been about developing the skills of teams of coaches, while Ann's focus was on making sure large school reform was happening. In other words Diane was advocating for coaches, and Ann was advocating for principals. It wasn't until they discussed writing this book that their perspectives began to change and grow. They acknowledged that sometimes their narrow view was getting in the way of making sure that coaching was working. Diane had to learn how coaching fits into the bigger school reform picture and not think of it as an isolated practice that would solve every problem. Ann had to learn that coaches were more than a "nice to have" role, but were critical in helping principals meet the teaching and learning demands in their school.

This book is a merging of both perspectives. It's not written for an audience of principal or for an audience of coach. It's written for both. While you may have previously read other books about student-centered coaching, this book takes a new stance by addressing the importance of the principal and coach partnership.

WHY THIS BOOK? WHY NOW?

We have encountered a variety of issues surrounding the principal and coach partnership. And even though we have varied backgrounds, it's interesting that the dilemmas are consistent across the K–12 schools where we work. If you have been involved in coaching, you've probably experienced some of these issues as well. Coaches trying to work around the principal, principals delegating too much to coaches, and coaches and principals working parallel rather than with each other. So much time, energy, and money are being expended with little impact. While this is often frustrating for teachers, the biggest losers are the students who miss out on deep, rich learning.

We have also found that in many districts there is a lack of support to principals regarding how to *lead* a coaching effort. This may be due to the simple fact that we haven't paid much attention to guiding principals through the rapid expansion of instructional coaching. We believe that when principals lack strategies for leading a coaching effort, they will encounter significant barriers to reaching their goal of positively impacting teaching and learning.

COACHING WITH THE BIG PICTURE IN MIND

Schools are complex systems. This complexity may lead us to try to do too many things at once. Lack of clarity results in people feeling confused, overwhelmed, and unsupported. The antidote to this confusion is to be thoughtful about what it is that you are going after, and then go after it with great intensity and focus.

One way we have learned to put the pieces together is to be clear about "the thing" we are trying to accomplish. This helps articulate how everything works together for the sake of student learning. Rather than wasting time and energy on unfocused efforts, schools can do better to align professional learning in service of student learning.

We like to use the following construct when thinking about how all the pieces fit together. *The thing* is whatever initiative your school has decided to implement. Examples include the implementation of the Gradual

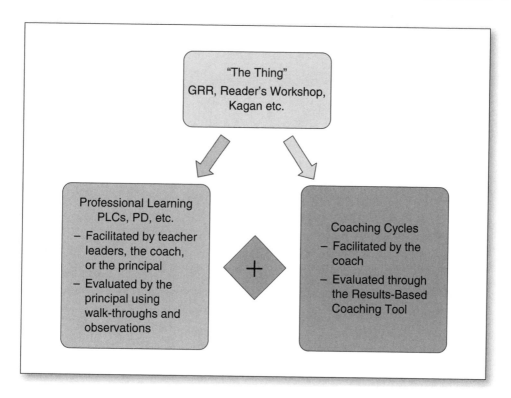

Release of Responsibility (GRR), Reader's Workshop, Kagan Strategies for Cooperative Learning, or Authentic Intellectual Engagement (AIW). There is no shortage of these types of initiatives in today's schools. The key is to select the thing that has the most potential to impact your students. What makes the thing come to life are the two supports that rest underneath: professional learning and coaching cycles. Both are equally important if these efforts are going to take root.

As you read through the graphic, you'll notice that professional learning includes collaboration (such as professional learning communities, learning teams, and department meetings) as well as large group professional development. In these sessions, teachers are engaged in learning that relates to instructional pedagogy. This learning is facilitated by teacher leaders, the coach, or the principal. These efforts are evaluated by the principal engaging in walk-throughs and observations in classrooms throughout the school. Imagine your "thing" is to decrease lecture and increase student discussion. It becomes apparent that professional learning must be delivered and evaluated if there is any hope of providing what teachers need.

Coaching cycles are an additional support that are facilitated by the coach, and may occur with individuals, pairs, or small groups. The impact of coaching cycles is monitored based on teacher and student learning. The in-depth support that is inherent in coaching cycles supports student learning while also reinforcing effective practices in the school improvement plan.

We have to keep in mind that coaching isn't an initiative (and that the coach isn't "the thing"). Rather it is an embedded support that helps all teachers meet the goals of the school. We view this as the intersection of school improvement, coaching, and most important learning, underscoring why the principal and coach relationship is so pivotal.

OUR INTENTIONS FOR THE CHAPTERS IN THIS BOOK

We chose to approach this book by tackling the toughest issues that are associated with integrating coaching into a school. Each chapter addresses a different aspect of building, sustaining, and learning from your coaching efforts. We provide practical ideas and solutions that can help you ensure that coaching is getting results.

With this in mind, we would recommend that you begin by building a solid understanding of the coaching model and strategies for school improvement (Chapters 1 and 2). After building this foundational knowledge, other chapters address common issues associated with leading coaching. Chapter 3 provides ideas and strategies to ensure that roles are clearly defined. In Chapter 4, you will learn how to integrate coaches in a way that contributes to a culture of learning. Creating a no opt culture is the focus of Chapter 5. All this rests on a clear understanding of what good instruction looks like, which is addressed in Chapter 6. Chapter 7 focuses on the perennial question of how to separate coaching from supervision. Finally, Chapter 8 addresses how to support coaches so they can continue to learn and grow.

In reading this book, we hope to create new intersections in how you think about coaching. We understand that leading a school isn't easy. That's all the more reason to learn how you can be more strategic about student-centered coaching. The story your school will tell rests on opening the doors and minds of your teachers and students. It is our hope that this book helps make this happen.

1 An Introduction to Student-Centered Coaching

"The work isn't done until every child benefits from the innovation."

—Nancy Mooney, District Leader

Instructional coaching has grown exponentially over the past two decades. Today there are coaches in large districts, small districts, urban districts, and rural districts. Coaches focus on subjects like mathematics, literacy, and technology. Others work across content areas. With millions of dollars and countless hours being dedicated to coaching, we must be sure that it is reaching the intended goal of increasing student and teacher learning.

Anything worth doing takes thoughtfulness, leadership, and a team approach. The same is true for coaching. While we often attribute the success of coaching to the skillfulness of the coach, the school leader is just as important to get the job done. The leader is essential because coaching is about lifting the learning of every member of the school community. We need everyone working together, taking risks, and committing to do what it takes to get there. At times, this may feel as challenging as lifting a 165,000 pound Space Shuttle off the ground. If you've seen the movie *The Right Stuff*, you may remember the scene when an astronaut is invited to join the team and he responds, "It sounds dangerous. Count me in." This is the sense of urgency that we are looking for when it comes to leading a coaching effort. We simply don't have time to waste. Although the astronaut's life was on the line, we are talking about the lives of our students. We believe that their success is just as important.

WHY IT MATTERS

Coaching Matters, and We Can Do Better

It is the principal's role to go beyond simply supporting a coaching effort. The principal must lead it. It takes a well-informed and strategic principal to do just that. While the principal is the key player, we recognize that there may be other district leaders who are instrumental in leading a coaching effort as well. For example, in a typical elementary school, the principal often leads the coaching effort. In a large comprehensive high school, an academic vice principal may be the one who guides the work. Sometimes a district leader is the point person on a coaching effort. For this reason, we will use the language *school leader* and *principal* as we speak to the instructional leaders who will ensure that coaching reaches the desired outcomes.

Strong leaders build partnerships with the coach, understand how to separate coaching from evaluation, and position the coach to be a valued resource within the school community. Yet many leaders receive very little direction regarding how to best deploy a coach. It's a familiar story: We hire great teachers out of the classroom and then assume that their instructional background will be enough to get them started as coaches. Would we hire nurses to perform complex surgeries and not train them to do so? Of course not. So why do we take this approach with coaching?

A recent meta-analysis focusing on how coaching impacts instructional practice makes this work all the more essential. According to Kraft, Blazar, and Hogan (2016),

> Turning to our primary meta-analytic results for instruction, we find large positive effects of coaching on teachers' instructional practice. We find a pooled effect size of .58 standard deviations (SD) across all 32 studies that included a measure of instructional practice as an outcome. (p. 20)

As advocates for coaching, we are thrilled to see the correlation between coaching and instructional practice. But we think there's more to do. We'd like to ensure that coaching directly impacts student achievement as well. This takes leadership. In the book *Reduce Change to Increase*

Improvement, Robinson (2018) writes, "Leadership is the enabler of improvement, orchestrating the various conditions, such as professional capability, community engagement, and quality instruction, that need to be working together if improvement in student outcomes is to be achieved and sustained" (p. 9).

Let's Remember: The Purpose of School Is Student Learning

It's easy to lose perspective on the fact that the purpose of school is student learning. This somewhat obvious notion is often lost as we develop and deliver a coaching model. We busily create all kinds of systems and structures. We provide professional learning opportunities, and we negotiate what we expect of teachers. With all these balls in the air, it's easy to forget our driving purpose. Kids don't go to school to participate in programs, they don't go to school to behave, and they don't go to school to score well on state tests. They go to school to learn.

We can so easily make coaching about student learning. When Diane began grappling with how to be more student-centered in her coaching, she was also studying *Understanding by Design* by Wiggins and McTighe (2005). It came together when she read, "We ask designers to start with a much more careful statement of the desired results—the priority *learnings*—and to derive the curriculum from the performances called for or implied in the goals" (2005, p. 17). This notion of working backward from the desired results became the operating principle of student-centered coaching.

This approach accomplished a few things. It became much easier to develop partnerships with teachers because the coach's role was to help the students reach the goals that had been set by the teacher. The impact was clearer because the teacher and coach would formatively assess student learning every step of the way. It also became easier to identify the growth that the teacher had made instructionally because it was nested in the context of teaching *and* learning.

Having a Coaching Model Is the First Step

It's incredible how many districts have coaches and no coaching model. A coaching model is a framework; it does not tell you how to coach or what to coach. A coaching framework is the underlying structure that you can use when you're coaching someone. Rostron (2009) writes,

> Coaching models help us to understand the coaching intervention from a systems perspective, and to understand the need for "structure"

in the interaction between coach and client. Models help us to develop flexibility as coach practitioners. They offer structure and an outline for both the coaching conversation and the overall coaching journey—whether it is for 20 hours, six months, a year or more. However, although models create a system within which coach and client work, it is imperative that models are not experienced as either prescriptive or rigid. (p. 116)

When a model is lacking, nobody really knows what coaches should be doing with their time. This can be downright confusing for members of the school community. Some teachers may worry that coaches will report their weaknesses back to the principal and that this information will be used in a punitive way. Others may assume that coaching only applies to teachers who are new or struggling. When school lacks a coaching model, the effort may become vague and has the potential to be a waste of resources. Here are some signs that a school is lacking a coaching model:

- Nobody knows the purpose for having a coach.
- Coaches aren't sure what they should be doing on a daily basis.
- Coaches don't receive guidance about how to organize and schedule their work.
- Coaches aren't provided with a clear process to follow when working with teachers.
- Coaches aren't sure who should participate in coaching cycles.
- There is no plan for measuring the impact of coaching.
- The coach is encouraged to "just build relationships" so that teachers won't be threatened.

The first step in determining the coaching model is deciding if coaching will be student-centered, teacher-centered, or relationship-driven. Figure 1.1 outlines each of these approaches based on a variety of factors. We find that starting here helps schools home in on their purpose for coaching.

Student-centered coaching is about partnerships where instructional coaches and teachers work together to reach their goals for student learning. This is a departure from a teacher-centered approach where the role of the coach is to implement a program or set of practices. Teacher-centered coaching may make sense when a school or district is adopting a new program or pedagogy because there are specific things a teacher may need to learn to implement. It can also be useful when new teachers need to learn how things are done in a school. The thing is, this approach can sometimes set the coach up to focus on what the teacher is—or isn't—doing. This may lead to the perception that the coach is there to hold teachers accountable

Figure 1.1 Coaching Continuum: Student-Centered, Teacher-Centered, and Relationship-Driven Coaching

More Impact on Students		Less Impact on Students

◄───►

	Student-Centered Coaching	Teacher-Centered Coaching	Relationship-Driven Coaching
Role	The coach partners with teachers to design learning that is based on a specific objective for student learning.	The coach moves teachers toward implementing a program or set of instructional practices.	The coach provides support and resources to teachers.
Focus	The focus is on using data and student work to analyze progress and collaborate to make informed decisions about instruction that is differentiated and needs-based.	The focus is on what the teacher is, or is not, doing and addressing it through coaching.	The focus is on providing support to teachers in a way that doesn't challenge or threaten them.
Use of Data	Formative assessment data and student work is used to determine how to design the instruction. Summative assessment data are used to assess progress toward standards mastery.	Summative assessment data are used to hold teachers accountable rather than as a tool for instructional decision making.	Data are rarely used in relationship-driven coaching.
Use of Materials	Textbooks, technology, and curricular programs are viewed as tools for moving student learning to the next level.	The use of textbooks, technology, and curricular programs is the primary objective of the coaching.	Sharing access and information to textbooks, technology, and curricular programs is the primary focus of the coaching.
Perception of the Coach	The coach is viewed as a partner who is there to support teachers to move students toward mastery of the standards.	The coach is viewed as a person who is there to hold teachers accountable for a certain set of instructional practices.	The coach is viewed as a friendly source of support who provides resources when needed.
Role of Relationships	Trusting, respectful, and collegial relationships are a necessary component for this type of coaching.		

Source: Sweeney, D. (2011). Student-Centered Coaching: *A Guide for K–8 Coaches and Principals.* Thousand Oaks, CA: Corwin. Used with permission.

or "fix" them. Or coaches may experience frayed relationships, or feel uncomfortable with being put in the position of "expert."

While nobody would argue that relationships are foundational to coaching, we don't want to only focus here. Relationship-driven coaching occurs when the coach focuses on providing teachers with resources and support. It often feels safer because the coach's role is about making the lives of teachers easier. When coaches face resistance, they may back off and settle for providing resources. We would argue that this form of coaching fails to get the desired results, and isn't a place we'd hope coaches would occupy for too long.

Considering these different approaches is a first step in establishing a coaching program. Does the principal want coaching to be squarely about implementation? Are student-outcomes the focus? Is the role of the coach to provide resources? Whatever the choice, it's important to recognize that over the years, coaching has been viewed with trepidation because teachers felt as if coaching was something that was "being done to them." According to Sweeney (2011),

> Coaching often centers exclusively on the actions taken by the teacher—making the assumption that if we improve the teaching, then student learning will improve as well. There is some logic to this approach, but unfortunately an unintended outcome is we've spent so much time thinking about what teachers *should* be doing that we've lost touch with the most important people in our schools . . . the students. (p. 8)

With so many schools lacking a coaching model, we thought we'd provide some ideas about how you might add clarity to a model that is being newly developed or revamped. We'd suggest taking the steps outlined in Figure 1.2.

WHAT IT LOOKS LIKE

In any coaching effort, it is the principal's role to design it, define it, and lead it. Organizational development guru Warren Bennis once said, "Leadership is the capacity to translate vision into reality" (Booher, 1992). This certainly applies to leading a coaching effort. Schools often start with a vision of using coaches to provide job-embedded support to teachers. That's a terrific vision that we would certainly endorse. But let's be honest that translating that vision into reality is where things become more challenging. The following moves are designed to help school leaders do just that.

Figure 1.2 Developing a Coaching Model

1. Commit to a student-centered approach to coaching.

2. Articulate your beliefs and commitments about coaching.

3. Define your process for coaching cycles.

4. Create a list of duties that coaches are engaged in on a daily or weekly basis.

5. Decide how you would like coaches to participate in teacher collaboration, such as professional learning communities (PLCs).

6. Develop a master schedule that includes common times for teachers to meet with the coach, a weekly principal and coach meeting, and collaboration time for teachers.

7. Decide how coaches will measure the impact of coaching on teaching and learning.

8. Plan how you will handle things that will potentially divert the coach's attention away from coaching cycles and toward administrivia (i.e., covering classrooms, organizing data, participating in every collaboration that occurs during any given week, etc.).

Leadership Move #1: Understand the Core Practices for Student-Centered Coaching

It's hard to lead something that you don't understand. If principals have any chance of ensuring that effective coaching is taking place, then they need to understand what effective coaching looks like. Figure 1.3 outlines the core practices for student-centered coaching.

Leadership Move #2: Expect Coaching Cycles

There is a real temptation to assign a laundry list of duties to coaches. This includes organizing assessment data, creating schedules for interventions, managing materials, or assigning other duties that don't align with the role of the coach. It is an especially common practice when a school has an undefined coaching model, because nobody's really sure what the coach should be doing in the first place. It might be the coach who seeks out busy work because it feels better to have something to do. The truth is, coaches who take on the broadest array of duties will be in fewer coaching cycles and, thus, will make less of an impact on student and teacher learning. (Read more about defining roles in Chapter 3.)

We know that one-shot opportunities for professional development do little to improve student learning. If coaches aren't engaged in coaching

Figure 1.3 Core Practices for Student-Centered Coaching

Core Practice	Purpose
1. Organize coaching through cycles	Coaching cycles create the conditions for a coach to make a lasting impact. If coaches work with teachers on an informal, or one-shot, basis, then the results will be diminished.
2. Set a standards-based goal for coaching cycles	Coaching that isn't standards-based often misses the point that school should be about learning. We frame coaching around learning by setting standards-based goals for coaching cycles.
3. Use student-friendly learning targets throughout the coaching cycle	Learning targets increase instructional clarity and provide a mechanism for better assessment by the teacher and more self-assessment by the students.
4. Use student evidence to co-plan instruction	Student evidence is used to drive decision making when planning lessons. This aligns with our belief that coaching ought to be built on a foundation of formative assessment.
5. Co-teach with a focus on effective instructional practices	Rather than modeling or observing, we advocate for coaches and teachers to build partnerships while working together in the classroom.
6. Measure the impact of coaching on student and teacher learning	It is our obligation to collect data to demonstrate how teachers and students are growing across coaching cycles.
7. Partner with the school leader	Without a solid partnership, the coach will not be in the position to make the desired impact.

cycles on a regular basis, then their coaching will be far less efficacious. We'd even go as far as to say that when coaching cycles are lacking, the coach is most likely in a relationship-driven mode. Principals often ask how much time should be spent in coaching cycles. We advocate for coaches to spend *most* of their time in cycles because it is the most results-based work that they will do. Coaching cycles include the following components:

- 4 to 6 weeks in duration
- Can occur with individuals, small groups, or pairs
- Include at least one weekly planning session
- Include between one to three co-teaching sessions each week

Leadership Move #3: Ask Teachers About Their Goals for Coaching Cycles

There may be nothing more affirming than for a school leader to understand and support the goals that teachers are working toward with a coach. We recommend for principals to ask teachers about their goals so that they can be sure to create conditions for the goal to be met. A principal recently modeled this during a conversation in the hallway. She said to the teacher, "I see that you are in a coaching cycle. Can you tell me a little about your goal for student learning?" The teacher responded, "Yes, we are working on narrative writing that ties to our social studies curriculum. I'm working with the coach and social studies team to make it work." The principal responded, "That's a great goal, and it is very much aligned with our vision for integration. I'd love to come into the classroom when you and the coach are working together. I can't wait to see what your students are able to do with their writing."

With this simple exchange, the principal did a few things. First, she sent a message that she valued and was interested in the work the teacher was doing with the coach. She also gained some quick insights into the teacher's vision when it came to her writing instruction. Last, she used this conversation as an opportunity to see the teacher and coach in action. A simple conversation led to a deeper (and shared) understanding of the work that was taking place.

It's also important to recognize that quality goals matter. We'd hate for a coach and teacher to spend 6 weeks on a goal that wasn't rigorous or aligned with the curriculum. Therefore, we seek goals that are (1) standards based, (2) valued by the teacher, (3) the right size and scope, (4) measurable through formative assessment, and (5) robust enough to carry a teacher and coach across a coaching cycle. Examples of goals for coaching cycles are detailed in Figure 1.4.

You'll notice that the examples of coaching cycle goals don't focus on implementing programs, such as, "Teacher will use the gradual release of responsibility during lessons." They aren't at the surface (or skills) level, such as, "Students will learn how to decode words using CVC sounds."

Figure 1.4 Examples of Goals for Coaching Cycles

Elementary Literacy	Students will use a variety of strategies to solve unknown words in texts.
Middle School Math	Students will understand and use ratios to make sense of real-world situations.
High School Economics	Students will understand how supply and demand impacts their life as a consumer.

Goals also don't simply focus on content, such as, "Students will learn the important battles of the Civil War." Rather, they are rigorous, interesting, and aligned with the standards. This is how we ensure that coaching takes learning deeper.

Leadership Move #4: Understand and Promote the Use of Learning Targets

Many school districts missed the point when it came to using learning targets to drive instruction. They focused on whether or not teachers posted them on the board rather than on they could be used to help students take ownership over the learning process. Moss, Brookhart, and Long (2011) reframe the use of learning targets when they write,

> Learning targets have no inherent power. They enhance student learning and achievement only when educators commit to consistently and intentionally sharing them with students. Meaningful sharing requires that teachers use the learning targets with their students and students use them with one another. This level of sharing starts when teachers use student-friendly language—and sometimes model or demonstrate what they expect—to explain the learning target from the beginning of the lesson, and when they continue to share it throughout the lesson. (p. 67)

Student-centered coaching embeds learning targets into every conversation. This increases teacher clarity around what the students should know and be able to do so that we can reach the goal. When teachers understand what mastery looks like, then they are more focused and deliberate in their teaching. Without learning targets, teachers are blind. With them they have a clear roadmap to follow. Figure 1.5 provides an

Figure 1.5 Example of Student-Friendly Learning Targets

Coaching Cycle Goal: Students will understand and use ratios to make sense of real-world situations.

- I can use ratio language to describe the relationship between two quantities.
- I can apply my understanding of unit rate to make sense of ratios.
- I can create and manipulate tables to compare ratios.
- I can solve unit rate problems.
- I can solve for the whole when given a part and the percentage.
- I can engage productively in small group work.

example of student-friendly learning targets that were used during a coaching cycle in a middle school math class.

Leadership Move #5: Build Student Evidence Into All Forms of Teacher Collaboration

We've lost sight of the types of assessment that matter. Checklists have taken over, and many teachers may not even know how their students are really doing. For this reason, student-centered coaching is rooted in the use of student evidence. Examples include: writing samples, reading responses, exit slips, open-ended math problems, anecdotal notes, and problem-solving tasks. It is the real work that students did that very day, and it is work that makes student learning visible.

If you were to audit collaboration and professional learning in your school, how often would student evidence be a part of the conversation? In most schools, the answer is rarely. While data, such as interim assessments or "scores" are commonly used, student evidence is often overlooked. This is a mistake because it means we aren't valuing formative assessments enough to use them during collaborative decision making. We'd even venture to guess that without being prioritized, formative assessment may not be happening much at all.

Carol Ann Tomlinson (2014) writes,

> It isn't really so much that these teachers use formative assessments *often*. It's that they do so *continually*—formally and informally, with individuals and with the group, to understand academic progress and to understand the human beings that they teach. For these teachers, formative assessment is not ancillary to effective teaching. It is the core of their professional work. (p. 10)

We recommend for school leaders to embed student evidence into as many collaborative conversations as possible. This sends the message that we base our decision making on where our students are rather than on what a colleague is doing or what the teacher may have found on Pinterest.

Leadership Move #6: Facilitate and Support Data Analysis

Student evidence is one piece of the puzzle. It serves the purpose of improving the methods and practices we use to formatively assess students. We also need to develop systems around higher level data, or summative assessments. Building this infrastructure is under the purview of the principal because these forms of data are one of our strongest levers for addressing concerns around student learning. Taking care to monitor student performance across the school year means that no students will fall through the cracks.

As a leading advocate for data-driven instruction, Paul Bambrick-Santoyo (2010) argues that all schools ought to be driven by data. He writes,

> Data-driven instruction is the philosophy that schools should constantly focus on one simple question: are our students learning? Using data-based methods, these schools break from the traditional emphasis on what teachers ostensibly taught in favor of a clear-eyed, fact-based focus on what students actually learned. (p. xxv)

There needs to be a clear distinction between the coach and principal when it comes to data that is used for the purposes of accountability. Coaches aren't in the role to lead these conversations because they are a tool for accountability rather than a tool for support. The reason for this is if we are using data teams to their full potential, then we are naming gaps in student performance and then taking action. Coaches aren't in the position to make teachers take action. Instead, they enter the picture when support is needed. Imagine a teacher who, through a data conversation, becomes aware that her students are at risk of not making a year's worth of growth as readers. Digging into this might become a meaningful goal for a coaching cycle. The key is for the coach to support the teacher to move student learning forward rather than looking for gaps in the teacher's performance. In this way, the coach and teacher honor their partnership and also work to execute the gaps that were surfaced through the data analysis.

Leadership Move #7: Keep Your Eye on Impact

A coach's biggest impact is made through coaching cycles, and coaching cycles must be measured. Otherwise we run the risk of implementing a coaching program with intangible results. As a school leader, expecting that coaching cycles are occurring is the first step. The second step is ensuring that they are being measured. We use the Results-Based Coaching Tool to understand how student and teacher learning were impacted. Figure 1.6 provides an overview of how we collect information when using the Results-Based Coaching Tool. We also included a template of the tool in Appendix E of this book.

We use the Results-Based Coaching Tool in many ways. Primarily, it is used to name and celebrate the growth that occurred as a result of coaching. If it is used as a "gotcha" tool, then teachers will begin to distrust the coaching process and steer clear. In Chapter 8, we provide ideas regarding

Figure 1.6   Measuring the Impact of a Coaching Cycle

At the Beginning of the Coaching Cycle	During the Coaching Cycle	At the End of the Coaching Cycle
Set a goal for student learning using the language, "Students will . . ."	Engage in weekly meetings to analyze student evidence and co-plan instruction.	Identify the instructional practices that the teacher is implementing on a regular basis.
After the goal is set, it is unpacked into student-friendly learning targets. This becomes the success criteria.	Work side by side to implement instructional practices that will support students to reach the goal.	Post assess to measure student performance in relationship to the goal for student learning. This provides growth data.
Pre assess to determine how they are doing in relation to the goal. This provides baseline data.	Continuously assess students using the learning targets.	Decide how to meet the needs of students who haven't reached mastery.

Source: Sweeney, D. (2011). *Student-Centered Coaching: A Guide for K–8 Coaches and Principals.* Thousand Oaks, CA: Corwin. Used with permission.

how a school leader can use the Results-Based Coaching Tool as a center-piece for providing feedback, support, and evaluation of coaches.

LESSON FROM THE FIELD

A Tale of Two Coaching Models

The following schools approached the launch of coaching in different ways. As you read their stories, consider the role that the principal played in introducing coaching to the faculty. Please note that the names of the schools were changed for the purposes of this book.

Emerson High School

Matt had been the principal at Emerson for several years and was known as the principal who left teachers to do their thing. He often shared that he got out of the way so that teachers could do their best work. Several teachers came to teach at Emerson because they had heard that the principal left you alone. Scott and Becky were hired from the teaching ranks to serve as technology integration coaches. Both were well liked by the staff. Matt hoped that this would smooth any discontent that may occur from having two new coaches in the school.

As they started the year, Scott and Becky reached out to Matt a few times to set up a planning meeting. It was hard to get it on his calendar and when they did meet, it was rushed. As new coaches, Scott and Becky felt like they were on their own to create the coaching model that would be used at Emerson. This was scary since they had never been coaches before. They also worried that they'd become enmeshed in supporting technology requests that didn't relate to learning in the classroom.

When they did finally meet, they asked Matt for guidance on how they would introduce themselves to the staff. He responded that they could share that they'll be "there for whatever the teachers needed." While they felt supported, it didn't feel like a plan. They wanted a plan.

Washington High School

Hugo and Amira were hired from the teaching ranks to serve as instructional coaches. Margaret was their principal and had a track record of fairness. When she learned that she would have two instructional coaches, her first step was to make sure she hired the right people for the job. Hugo was a well-regarded math teacher. Amira was a respected English Language Arts teacher who had been in the school for over 10 years.

Margaret acknowledged that in the past the school had used a teacher-centered coaching model, and she wanted the teachers to understand that this year would be different. To support this shift, she made sure to schedule regular meetings with the coaches. During these meetings, they would discuss how coaching was going and what she could do to help them take their work further. In their first meeting, they created a chart titled, "'What Coaching Is and Isn't" (Figure 1.7). Their plan was to share what they created at the first staff meeting.

When they introduced coaching to the staff, Margaret shared the chart, "What Coaching Is and Isn't." She focused on the belief that coaching was about helping teachers reach their goals for student learning. She also shared that she would be working closely with Hugo and Amira and that they would be seeking teacher feedback every step of the way. Teachers got the message loud and clear—this was important.

What Can We Learn From These Examples?

Leaving things to chance is not the way to get coaching off on the right foot. Margaret took ownership over the process so that there would be clarity among teachers about what coaching is and why it's important. This set up the coaches for success. When coaches are left to go it alone, they will struggle. This is not only unfair to the coaches but to the system as a whole. Why waste this precious resource?

Figure 1.7 What Coaching Is and Isn't

Coaching Is	Coaching Isn't
A partnership	Evaluative
Focused on student learning	Focused on making teachers do things
Good for our students	About fixing teachers
Outcomes and standards-based	A waste of time
Driven by teachers' goals	Driven by the administrator, coach, or district
Flexible and responsive	Fixed and inflexible
Fun and interesting	Something to avoid

WHERE ARE YOU NOW?

The following self-assessment focuses on the skills and understandings that principals must build if they choose to implement student-centered coaching. Each chapter includes a self-assessment of this kind. In this chapter, we support the principal to develop an understanding of student-centered coaching to lead the effort.

Figure 1.8 Self-Assessment for School Leaders

Understand the Philosophy and Methods for Student-Centered Coaching			
	Accomplished	**Developing**	**Novice**
The School Leader	The principal understands the core practices for student-centered coaching, subscribes to these practices, and provides support to move coaching forward. The principal provides the necessary pressure and support to ensure that coaching is used to its full potential.	The principal has some knowledge of the core practices for student-centered coaching, may question its value, or may not be actively involved in the coaching effort. The principal is beginning to find a balance between providing the adequate pressure and support to ensure that coaching is used to its full potential.	The principal is not supportive of, lacks knowledge in, or takes a passive approach to supporting the implementation of the core practices for student-centered coaching. The principal focuses on either pressure or support rather than finding a balance between the two. Coaching is not used to its full potential.

(Continued)

(Continued)

	Accomplished	Developing	Novice
Success Criteria	I can . . . • Support the coach to effectively use the core practices for student-centered coaching. • Organize the schedule to make time for coaching to occur. • Facilitate data collection and use data in collaborations, such as PLCs. • Create the infrastructure for regular data analysis. • Avoid using coaching in a punitive manner. • Supervise and support teachers who are at risk rather than asking the coach to do so.		

Troubleshooting Around Implementation of Student-Centered Coaching

We often hear from coaches and school leaders that they wish they had started with more clarity around their coaching model. The saying "Hindsight is 20/20" applies here because it's easy to go down the road of implementing coaching before the pieces are in place. If you are in this situation, here are some ideas to get coaching back on track (Figure 1.9).

Figure 1.9 Language for Supporting the Coaching Effort

If I hear . . .	Then I can say . . .
"Can't I just meet with the coach a few times?"	"We value coaching cycles because they provide the greatest impact. It takes more than a few coaching sessions to see it pay off with the students. That's what we want to focus on."
"Our teachers are overwhelmed, so this year we are going to focus on building relationships."	"I understand that there is a lot going on. But remember that our coaching model is based on helping students grow. Let's work to find out what is causing teachers to be overwhelmed and then the school leadership team can wrestle with those issues. We want to make sure our coaches stay focused on helping support student learning."
"I'm not sure what to expect from coaching, so I think I'll steer clear."	"Coaching as a student-centered practice that is all about helping you reach your goals for student learning. Let's talk about the differences between student-centered, teacher-centered, and relationship-driven coaching. That way you'll know what to expect."

THE COACH'S ROLE

While it is vital for the principal to support the use of the core practices for student-centered coaching, it's up to the coach to develop the skills they need to use them. If we had to pick a few things for a coach to focus on, these would be what we'd recommend. For more on these coaching moves, please read *Student-Centered Coaching: The Moves* (Sweeney & Harris, 2016).

Set the Right Goals

The goal-setting process is how we set up coaching to be student-centered. It is a pivotal part of the process, and we find that if the goal isn't "just right" then the coaching cycle may go sideways. A few areas to pay attention to when setting goals are:

Goal Setting for Coaching Cycles

- Is the goal focused on a standard?
- Is the goal challenging and rigorous for students?
- Is the goal just right (not too broad and not too narrow)?
- Does the teacher care about the goal?

Use Student Evidence in Planning Conversations

Coaches work with teachers to sort student work according to trends and then deliver differentiated instruction that matches exactly where the students are on any given day. Using student evidence provides the coach with the opportunity to help teachers make informed instructional decisions. We find it less useful to frame coaching around data such as interim or summative assessments. While assessments of this nature are important for a school system, they don't often inform the day-to-day decision making of teachers. Therefore, when using student evidence, we focus on written responses, open-ended problem solving tasks, responses to reading, anecdotal or conference notes, and anything else that makes the students' learning visible.

Remember That Coaching Also Happens in the Classroom

When we think about coaching, our first impulse is to expect the coach to model lessons. The problem is modeling doesn't go very far in building partnerships with teachers. Rather, we advocate for coaches to spend most of their time co-teaching. The following practices provide techniques that a coach can use working in classrooms with teachers (Figure 1.10).

Figure 1.10 Co-Teaching Moves

Coaching Move	What It Looks Like
Noticing and Naming	During the lesson, the teacher and coach focus on how the students are demonstrating their current understanding in relation to the learning targets. As we work with students, we will record student evidence that we will use in our planning conversations.
Thinking Aloud	The teacher and coach share their thinking throughout the delivery of a lesson. By being metacognitive in this way, we will be able to name successes and work through challenges in real time.
Teaching in Tandem	The teacher and coach work together to co-deliver the lesson. The lesson is co-planned to ensure the roles are clear, that the learning targets are defined, and that we both understand how the lesson is crafted.
You Pick Four	The teacher identifies four students whom the coach will focus on when collecting evidence. The coach keeps the learning targets in mind while collecting student evidence. This evidence is then used in future planning conversations.
Micro Modeling	A *portion* of the lesson is modeled by the coach. The teacher and coach base their decision about what is modeled on the needs that have been identified by the teacher.

Source: Sweeney, D., & Harris, L. (2016). *Student-Centered Coaching: The Moves.* Thousand Oaks, CA: Corwin. Used with permission.

IN CLOSING

As coaching expands, so does the importance of garnering consistent results across schools. While we find some schools that leverage coaching to impact teacher and student learning, we find others that are struggling to make the same growth. The most successful schools have developed a strong partnership between the principal and coach. Without a solid principal and coach partnership, the impact of coaching is minimized.

Many principals receive very little support when it comes to leading a coaching effort. This may be due to the fact that instructional coaching has gone through a rapid expansion over that past decade. It's also challenging because schools are complex and difficult places to enact change.

But even with all this complexity, we can't leave it up to the coaches to lift the learning of the schools on their own. This leaves coaches feeling overwhelmed and unsupported. Give these coaches a few years, and they'll head straight back to the classroom. How about if instead we doubled down on the principal and coach partnership? This will allow us to get much more out of a coaching effort. When the principal and coach are working as a team, the sky's the limit. Much like it was for those astronauts who decided to take a risk and go for it.

2

Connecting School Improvement to Coaching

"Always remember, your focus determines your reality."

—George Lucas

A clear and focused plan for improving student outcomes is as essential to principals as blueprints are to architects. Imagine building a house and having workers (i.e., plumbers, carpenters, and electricians) show up and do whatever they want to do. This sounds crazy, because it is. And yet this is what we do to coaches and teachers when they work in schools without a well-articulated school improvement plan. Builders use a detailed blueprint that outlines what the structure will look like when it is completed. The plan provides direction and guidance so that everyone involved knows and understands what they are building. Building schools is no different.

Developing a strong school improvement and professional development (PD) plan leverages coaching efforts because it helps everyone in the school, especially principals and coaches, stay focused on what matters most. With the plethora of information coming at a school leader every day, it is easy to get distracted by quick fix programs or the razzle dazzle of a new initiative. The only way to avoid this trap is to be clear on what is being built and then to build it. Like the foreman and construction worker, principals and coaches work together to make sure that plans are implemented so student learning flourishes. Coaches make the plan work because they help close the knowing/doing gap around the school's initiatives. Building a structure that stands the test of time requires planning and skilled workers. Improving a school is no different. What is critical in both instances is that everyone works together around a clear focus and vision.

WHY IT MATTERS

When it comes to understanding the urgency of using focused school improvement processes, we can take a lesson from geese. Geese fly in a V formation because this provides each bird with additional lift and reduces air resistance for the bird flying behind it. By flying in this formation the whole flock can fly 70% further with the same amount of energy required for one goose to fly alone. They can fly further, faster, and with less energy, ensuring that they reach their destination intact. Geese have a clear destination, and they organize themselves so that they inherently help each other make it to the finish line.

When schools have a clear picture of where they are headed, they can align resources to make sure they reach their destination. They can make certain the coaches are in the correct formation lifting and leading others so students can take flight. To inspire a sense of urgency, a former superintendent of Ann's used to say, "Our students only get one chance at this school year." We don't have the luxury in schools to squander our most valuable resource, which is time. Having a clear plan that aligns to the mission, vision, and needs of the school helps create a culture that allows everyone to thrive because it creates a shared sense of purpose and builds a continuous improvement mindset, which both lay the groundwork for coaching.

Improvement Requires a Systems Approach

The work of improving a school or district requires a systems approach. Research has proven time and time again that sustained improvement for all students occurs when a school or system has a tight instructional focus (Elmore, 2004; Fullan & Quinn, 2016). When schools focus on the right things and stay with them, lasting and remarkable success happens. Systems that build a common language and knowledge base along with implementing proven pedagogical practices outperform schools that do not have this focus (Robinson, 2011).

The path to improving a system requires a shared depth of understanding about the purpose and nature of the work by all individuals in the system, what Fullan and Quinn (2016) call coherence. Coherence happens when there is clarity of purpose, precision in practice, transparency, monitoring of progress, and continuous correction. Coherence requires purposeful actions and interactions. Picture those classrooms where teachers have clear and specific learning targets that guide their teaching. Students know what these are, and the entire classroom is working toward meeting these outcomes. The term *well-oiled machine* comes to mind when you spend time in these environments. Schools that experience coherence are acting in the same manner. There are clear benchmarks for the school, and the entire staff is working together to meet these goals through learning and collaboration. Just as learners struggle in classrooms that are chaotic, so do teachers in schools that lack coherence. It is hard for the work of student-centered coaching to make a lasting impact if teachers feel fragmented and unsure of the work they are doing.

Capacity Building Is Critical to Improving a System

To get beyond rhetoric, and get to deep levels of implementation, leaders need to build collective capacity. "Collective capacity building involves the increased ability of educators at all levels of the system to make the instructional changes required to raise the bar and close the gap for all students" (Fullan & Quinn, 2016, p. 57). The goal is for everyone in the system to have the necessary knowledge and skills, not just one or two superstar teachers. For this type of shift to occur, it takes more than all hands on deck, it takes an all hands rowing in the same direction. Avoiding role redundancies between the principal and coach is necessary for moving forward. Without this, principals and coaches can find themselves tripping over each other and wasting time and energy.

Capacity building requires attention to both individual and collective practice. Student-centered coaches provide support at both levels through one-on-one and small group coaching. Improving instructional practice is difficult work, but coaches who are provided the time and space to do the nitty gritty work of coaching (digging deep into analyzing student work to adjust practice) are critical drivers in enhancing the collective capacity of the school. Coaches aren't "the thing" as referenced in the introduction; coaches are what makes the thing happen by helping everyone in the school improve student outcomes through building capacity.

Metacognition Is Necessary to Improve Practice

The goal of professional learning in schools is not only to help teachers improve practice in the here and now, but to help them understand why the practice works so that they will use it again. To borrow from psychology, we want to help teachers be consciously competent (Burch, 1970). This is the third of four stages of competence that relate to the psychological states involved in the process of learning something new. Individuals move from not knowing what they don't know to being so competent that the skill has become second nature. At the consciously competent stage the individual knows or understands something; however, demonstrating the skills or knowledge requires concentration. Executing the new learning requires heavy conscious involvement. The reason scripted lessons and step-by-step teaching manuals don't work is because they dismiss this critical point. A hallmark of learning is when the learner can apply "the stuff" they have learned to new and unique situations. This involves synthesizing new information and comparing to existing understanding to make meaning. It requires a system of support that helps teachers wrestle with and apply their new learning. How can we expect teachers to get to a consciously competent stage if we don't give them the time they need to learn?

Higher order thinking uses more of our brain's capacity. Analyzing, critiquing, and redesigning all require a heavy cognitive load. This is why we need coaches. As palpable as our brains are, the resources are limited. When attention is paid to one thing, there is less capacity for everything else. The more attention we pay to everything, the less discerning we become. Focusing isn't just efficient, it leaves us better able to use the knowledge that we have gained. It allows us to think. Distractions impede thinking. Schools that have clearly articulated school improvement and professional plans outperform schools that don't because they minimize distractions, allowing teachers space to concentrate and think about improving a small number of practices. Student-centered coaches are a critical asset in cultivating a culture of thinking, learning, and growing, but are hindered in their efforts if a school is all over the place regarding instructional demands.

Schools Are Complex Systems

A principal we work with frequently says, "It's not one thing, it's everything." This may sound counterintuitive after the previous sections, but schools are complex systems, which means they are made up of interconnected parts. The interdependence inherent in a system results in a ripple effect; one thing is touched, and other parts of the system are affected.

Mausbach and Morrison (2016) use the analogy of a garden to illustrate this interconnectedness. A gardener avoids counterproductive practices like putting plants that need shade in spots where they get full sun. They figure out how to have the parts of the system (soil, seeds, and weather conditions) work in concert rather than in competition.

School leaders must think in similar terms. Figuring out how all the parts of the system work together to help students grow must be priority number one for school leaders. This is why clearly discerning the differences between the coach and principal roles and responsibilities is so critical. Without this clear distinction, principals and coaches can unwittingly engage in practices that are counterproductive and hinder system growth. A core function of system leadership is translating the vision of the organization into a reality by setting a direction that results in whole school consistency and high expectations (Leithwood, Day, Sammons, Harris, & Hopkins, 2006). This requires a keen understanding of both the whole and the parts in the system.

WHAT IT LOOKS LIKE

Connecting coaching to school improvement efforts begins with the principal understanding the connection between school improvement processes. Armed with this understanding the principal can then work to make sure that coaching efforts are connecting to and supporting school improvement efforts so deep levels of implementation can occur. The leadership moves identified in the next section provide practical guidance to make this happen.

Leadership Move #1: Align School Improvement Processes

Just as cars veer off the road without proper alignment, so it is for schools that fail to connect school improvement processes. Mooney and Mausbach (2008) identify five core processes that they refer to as *blueprint processes* for school improvement. These processes are as follows:

1. Establishing a mission, vision, and values that guide the general direction of the school and it's future actions;

2. Using data analysis, which includes both collecting and interpreting data for decision making;

3. Using a school improvement plan to guide goals, strategies, action steps, and decisions to create a working plan for the school;

4. Implementing professional development that serves as the engine for the school improvement plan; and

5. Differentiating supervision of teaching and learning to monitor how processes are working in classrooms.

Alignment of school improvement is when all the processes (mission and vision, data, the plan, professional development, and supervision) work in concert (Mooney & Mausbach, 2008). It is the interconnectedness of these processes that determines the success of the school. Cars run best when all the parts are in tune and working together. The same holds true for schools, if one of the core processes is missing, for example differentiated supervision of the plan, then the journey for improvement may hit a detour or be in for a very bumpy ride. Figure 2.1 provides an overview of the processes and their relationship.

Alignment happens when the leader has the mindset that everything in the organization is instrumental to the achievement of collective goals. Rather than looking outside the organization for improvement levers, leaders look within and work to align the processes and resources in a systematic and focused way (Elmore, 2008). Using the mission to help determine what data to collect, identifying professional development practices based on the strategies in the school improvement plan, and using look fors to determine what to observe in classrooms are examples of how these processes help leaders look from within. Each process requires the leader to collaborate with staff to make decisions about the direction of the school. Decisions made throughout the cycle of school improvement have a direct impact on how resources will be used and how staff work together.

Many times, schools and districts believe they have alignment because they have several of these processes in place. For example, a mission statement may exist or schools may have improvement plans and engage in data analysis. However, these processes are done in isolation of each other and are treated as separate activities rather than as actions that must interosculate to get maximum results. Misalignment is so detrimental because it perpetuates the "silo" mentality that is far too rampant in many schools. Silos get created because there isn't a shared sense of purpose on what and how to do the work. Overcoming isolationism requires leaders to take alignment issues head on. Figure 2.2 outlines some common problems with alignment and actions leaders can take to address these problems.

Alignment is a key factor to maximizing coaches' effectiveness because it helps create a shared mindset. It keeps the focus on promoting positive teacher, coach, and principal relationships since everyone is working

Figure 2.1 Blueprint Processes for School Improvement

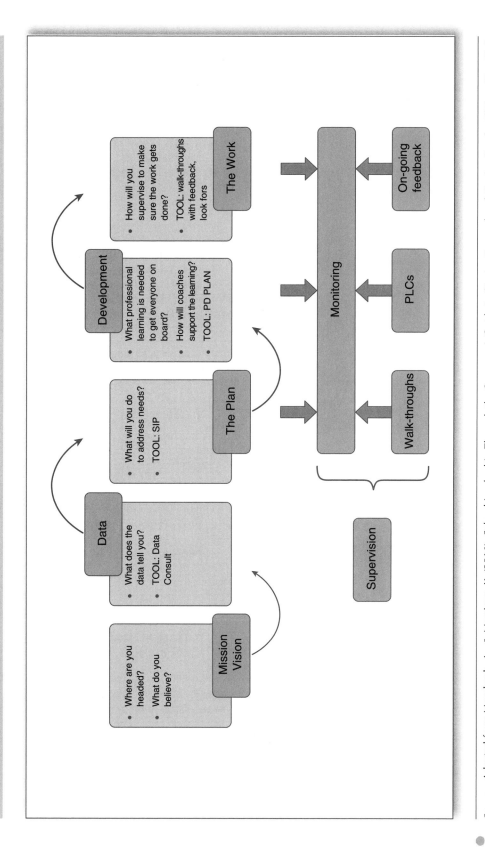

Source: Adapted from Mausbach, A., & Morrison, K. (2016). *School Leadership Through the Seasons: A Guide to Staying Focused and Getting Results All Year.* New York, NY: Routledge.

Figure 2.2   Common Alignment Problems and Solutions

Problem	Principal Actions to Address
Addressing mission and vision only at the beginning of each school year	• Refer to the mission and vision when engaging in school improvement work. • Highlight examples of the mission in action throughout the year. • Use the mission as a touchstone when making decisions.
Using annual data analysis versus continuous data analysis for decision making	• Distribute data as they become available followed by analysis and collective interpretation. • Clearly identify data points in the school improvement plan that help measure impact on student learning, and then collect this data on an ongoing basis and share progress with staff. • Establish collaboration, such as professional learning communities (PLCs), that uses student data as the cornerstone for the work.
Treating development of a school improvement plan as a one-time event driven by compliance to an outside source (i.e., district office, accreditation agency)	• Use school data to determine areas for improvement. • Identify both implementation and impact data points, collect on an ongoing basis, and revise plan as needed throughout the year.
Developing professional development plans that are selected and governed by persons outside the school Creating professional development plans that are loosely related to the school improvement plan	• Develop professional development around identified needs of the school from the school improvement plan. • Actively participate in PD and PLCs. • Create an infrastructure for learning in the school that promotes both large and small group learning. • Resist trainings, programs, or initiatives that are not a part of the strategies in the school improvement plan.
Supervising teachers using daily monitoring methods that are not connected to the school improvement or professional development plan	• Set clear expectations regarding frequent classroom visitation for the purpose of monitoring teaching and learning in addition to evaluation of teachers. • Collaboratively develop clear look fors around the school's initiatives so everyone understands what implementation looks like and sounds like.

Source: Adapted from Mooney & Mausbach (2008).

toward the same desired state. Having a clear plan for improvement helps teachers see that the coach is a partner in the journey. It also removes the hurdle of using formative assessment data during coaching cycles because using data and looking at student work is a common practice across the school. An aligned system promotes a continuous growth mindset, which is just the type of environment coaches need to thrive.

Leadership Move #2: Think Skinny When Planning ✕

"We can't put one more thing on their plate" is a frequent mantra in today's schools. As well intentioned as this sentiment is, it unwittingly communicates one dimensional thinking. Schools are complex systems with many parts. It is unrealistic to think that there won't be more than one thing on the plate. How unhealthy would it be if we just ate one thing every day? The key isn't taking things on or off as much as it is in portion control. So while there may be more than one thing on the plate, the amount of what is on the plate needs adjusting based on what is best for the school. Think more vegetables, less starch. The trick is to boil down the change into the smallest number of key high yield factors that have impact on learning, Fullan's notion of "skinny" (2009).

To get "skinny," leaders need to think in terms of "simplexity" (Kluger, 2009). *Simplexity* means the plans are less than complex, but not overly simple. Three key practices aid in development of a skinny plan that integrates coaching, engages staff, and improves outcomes for students. (See Appendix C for an example of a student-centered school improvement plan.)

Use Clear and Deliberate Language

Schools and school systems are highly compartmentalized both by physical and organizational design. Teachers in the science wing may rarely interact with the fine arts wing, not only because they are physically separated, but also because the school schedule does not allow for common planning or lunch times. This isolation hampers reform efforts and adds to confusion or disengagement, complicating coaching efforts since they work with a variety of teachers across the school. Because this isolation exists it is important to use common language so that everyone is on the same page. Figure 2.3 outlines questions and language that create shared meaning and clarity for leaders, coaches, and teachers.

Limit the Number of Goals and Strategies

This may seem like common sense, but in our experience working with a variety of schools in diverse settings, this tends to be one of the biggest problems with improvement plans. If the purpose of having goals is to determine direction, then having five or more goals means five or more destinations, which can put the school on divergent paths. One useful way to help limit goals is to keep them centered on student outcomes. Then strategies are

Figure 2.3 Questions and Language for Developing a School Improvement Plan

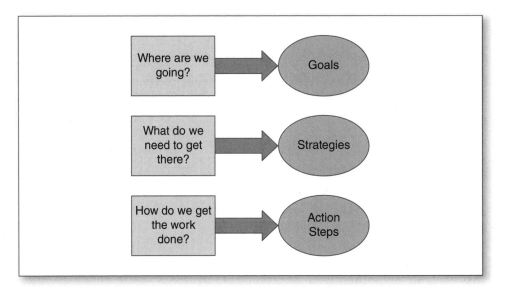

about the work of the adults to help meet the goal. For example, one goal area may be to improve achievement. Under this goal there may be two strategies such as to implement formative assessments and improve feedback practices to students. On the surface these goals and strategies seem simple, it is in the execution that complexity enters the picture.

One of the biggest challenges of keeping the plan skinny is the multitude of initiatives coming from either the district or the state. Schools must align themselves with district initiatives; however, blindly complying with demands from higher-ups can sabotage real reform efforts. Just as we advocate for coaches to work closely with building principals, so should principals work with central office staff. Central to making this relationship work is the understanding that all parties want the same thing, and that is to see progress or growth. When addressing district mandates, principals need to work in partnership with the district office to determine what aspects of the initiative make the most sense for the context of their school in that moment in time. District leaders also are also wise to think skinny when rolling out new initiatives. This means limiting both the number and the pace of new reform efforts.

Use Professional Development Needs as the Barometer

The best indicator about whether or not the goals, strategies, and action steps in the school improvement plan are doable is to take a close look at the professional learning needs that stem from the plan. Listing all the things teachers would need to know and be able to do if the strategies were implemented by the entire staff provides a realistic picture of the likelihood of the success of the plan. If the plan requires teachers to learn a long list of new practices, then the plan is too big. Can every single teacher in the school take on everything that is listed? Many times that answer is no, so scale back. Just as the barometric meter alerts us about changes in weather conditions so we can react appropriately, the amount of professional learning required in plans serves as an indicator of the reasonableness of improvement efforts. It alerts us to whether there will be stormy times ahead (asking teachers to learn too many new things at once) or sunny days (giving teachers the time and space to learn a limited number of high leverage practices).

Leadership Move #3: Collaboratively Develop the Plan

So many times the term *buy-in* surfaces when talking about getting staff to engage in reform efforts. True engagement, however, requires a deeper level of commitment, it requires ownership. Leaders can't force this type of commitment, rather their influence lies in the environment they create (Senge, 2006). Staff are unable to own initiatives if they aren't a part of the process. This process requires principals to walk a fine line between getting bogged down taking an inordinate amount of time to develop the plan versus having staff simply sign off on the documents. Leaders navigate this fine line by creating an infrastructure that allows all staff to systematically provide input and review progress.

The concept of a leadership team isn't new to schools; however, these teams typically address a variety of issues throughout the school. Tapping into a leadership team enables the principal and coach to get relevant input from teachers. In this way, school improvement and professional learning are a priority, and in turn, create a guiding vision for the coach.

According to Mausbach and Morrison (2016) the number of teams will vary depending on the size of the school, but as a rule of thumb all instructional staff need to be engaged in school improvement planning. Teachers should be able to select a goal area and work with that team. It is the principal's role to ensure that all staff members are represented on teams. For example, if a teacher is interested in math, she would serve on the team that is spearheading the work in this goal area. A member from each goal team would also serve on the overall school leadership team. This ensures that information developed and reviewed during team meetings can be shared throughout the school. The key is to have a structure and then to put the issues of school improvement as the focus of the agenda.

Leadership Move #4: Layer Professional Learning

Nancy Mooney, co-author of *Align the Design* (2008), used to say that professional development is the engine of school improvement. It is what makes the plan move forward. The goal for professional learning is to improve outcomes for students. For this to happen teachers need to transfer and apply learning to the real-life situations that occur in their classrooms. This won't happen if professional learning is treated as an event that is disconnected from the goals, strategies, and action steps in the school improvement plan. We use the term *layer* when it comes to professional learning because it evokes a mental picture of providing more than one thing at the same time. The key is to blanket teachers with the support they need to learn and grow. This requires multiple opportunities to learn in multiple ways. Figure 2.4 outlines the structures needed, benefits, and what it looks like at each layer. Sweeney (2011) refers to these as the Three Venues of Professional Development.

These structures have the greatest impact when the leader is intimately involved. Observations, feedback, and active participation in collaboration, such as PLCs, must be the routine work of the principal. The constant and consistent presence in classrooms and PLCs provides a principal with

Figure 2.4 Layers of Professional Learning

	Why Needed	Benefits	What It Looks Like
Large Group	• Helps everyone hear the same message at the same time • Helps develop shared meaning	Efficient way to share new concepts especially when launching a new initiative or practice	• Faculty professional development • Feedback letters to entire staff providing insights from walk-throughs • Conferences and workshops
Small Group	Provides additional time to wrestle with applying new learning in context	• Promotes transfer of learning from workshop to classroom • Builds collective capacity	• Grade level team • Inquiry team • Planning team • Interdisciplinary team • Intervention team
One-on-One	Refine practice	Builds self-efficacy	• Coaching cycles • Feedback conversations with principal

real-time information about what is working in the school and allows them to work in partnership with the coach. This focus helps everyone but especially coaches because it removes the burden from them being the primary eyes and ears of instruction. Observations and feedback help the leader discern if PD efforts are on track or if additional supports are needed. Think of how ludicrous it would be for a football coach to try to improve the team's record without showing up for a game. Yet this is what happens when principals take a hands-off approach to school improvement efforts. Ensuring quality teaching is happening for every student in the building requires a leader who is present and continually monitoring the instructional program with an eye on coherence.

LESSON FROM THE FIELD

It was Garry's 5th year as the principal of a high-poverty elementary school. Student achievement had improved since his tenure, but Garry and his staff weren't satisfied with the results. Using their recently revised mission, which highlighted collaboration, the school improvement team dug in and decided to take an honest look at how PLCs were working in the school. A staff survey indicated that although student work was consistently being examined, teams were getting mired in determining proficiency rather than identifying actions to address the students' needs. These data matched what both Garry and the coaches had observed when they attended weekly grade-level PLCs.

The focus of their plan shifted to using interim assessment data because this would provide much needed information about students' progress on the standards and would provide a unifying process that everyone in the school could use to help them respond to student needs.

After determining this focus, Garry and the two coaches (one math, one literacy) decided to provide more support to teachers so that the assessment data generated would be used to plan instruction. To do this they devised a two-step process for PLCs that consisted of a (1) preplanning protocol and a (2) review and action protocol.

The preplanning protocol was used during the principal and coach meetings just after the interims had been administered. Garry and the coaches reviewed grade-level data and identified strengths and areas for growth based on the standards that were being assessed. With this information in mind, they strategically gathered resources that they felt might be useful when the grade-level team unpacked the data during the upcoming PLC. For example, when the 2nd-grade students were struggling with the standard of counting up and over 100, the math coach brought examples of ideas of how to use manipulatives while Garry brought a short excerpt from a Van De Walle, Karp, and Bay-Williams (2012) book on math instruction.

The Review and Action Protocol was used during the 45-minute long PLC meeting. This consisted of the team using a timed whip around (3–5 minutes) that consisted of three rounds. During Round One, the team identified which standards or concepts were strengths. Round Two consisted of identifying areas of growth. The final round consisted of sharing strategies teachers could use to teach the concepts that needed work. If needed, additional time was added so they could make sure that the team "got everything out" regarding practices that would help teach the concept. Garry acted as the timekeeper during the protocol, and the coach was an active participant, sharing alongside the teachers.

After the team had created a list of ideas, they spent the rest of the time identifying three to four realistic strategies and actions, and then prioritized which ones they would implement first. During this portion of the meeting, the coach was often asked to explain or model what the strategy might look like in the classroom. Teachers who wanted additional support also requested coaching cycles.

While a bit clunky at first, especially if teachers hadn't looked at their data prior to the meeting, after a few months, the process was clicking. As a result, teachers felt that the PLCs were more productive because they left with concrete ideas of things to do to address student needs, the coaches felt embedded in the process of helping students meet standards, and best of all student achievement improved.

WHERE ARE YOU NOW?

Developing and implementing school improvement plans that improve outcomes for students requires attention to critical leadership practices. It also sets the coach up for success because there is a clear roadmap to follow. We suggest using the following rubric to self-assess and set goals around these important leadership moves (Figure 2.5).

Troubleshooting Around Developing and Connecting Coaching to School Improvement Efforts

Maintaining the focus on improving outcomes for students is difficult, especially if the school culture is not used to having a clear plan that aligns professional learning and resources around goals and strategies. Staying the course requires sending a consistent message about the school's focus

Figure 2.5 Self-Assessment for School Leaders

Develop Systems for Professional Learning and Coaching			
	Accomplished	**Developing**	**Novice**
The School Leader	The school leader aligns professional development and coaching to schoolwide goals and initiatives. This creates a focus for teacher development and student learning.	The school leader is working to establish a focus for teacher development and student learning. The school leader may be challenged to prioritize or stay the course with the school improvement effort.	The school leader doesn't create a PD plan that is executed on. This creates an unfocused professional development environment.
	There is a well-designed PD plan that includes large group, teacher teams, and individualized support for teachers.	The PD plan isn't used to its full potential. It lacks connections between large group, teacher teams, and individualized support for teachers.	There are many topics covered when it comes to PD. There aren't connections made between large group, teacher teams, and individualized support for teachers.
Success Criteria	I can . . . • Work with the coach and teacher leaders to create a student-centered SIP and PD plan • Execute the plan by revisiting it during the principal and coach meetings • Use data to guide SIP, PD, and coaching • Make connections between large group, teacher teams, and individualized support for teachers • Listen and adapt the plan based on student performance and teacher feedback		

and how resources will be used. Figure 2.6 provides language to support principals through these conversations.

THE COACH'S ROLE

It's hard to imagine how schools can improve the performance of all students without student-centered coaches. Coaches link the schoolwide student goals to the classroom through coaching cycles that focus on outcomes. Their actions and interactions can help or hinder the focus of the school, which is why they need to be cognizant of the weight their role carries in the overall improvement of the school.

Figure 2.6 Language for Keeping School Improvement Efforts Focused on Students

If I hear . . .	Then I can say . . .
"Why are we still working on this? Wasn't this a part of our plan last year?"	"This was a part of the plan last year, but you may remember when we took a look at both our implementation and student achievement data, we still had work to do. The great thing about maintaining our focus is that we can deepen our learning from last year."
"Why are the coaches sharing resources around the strategies in our school improvement plan? I need help planning lessons."	"As you know the coaches' job is varied, but one of their roles is to support us in our efforts to meet student outcomes. By providing resources that support our strategies, the coaches are helping us meet the school's goals. This doesn't mean they can't help you meet student goals in your classroom. This might not look like traditional lesson planning, but together I am sure the two of you could develop some great strategies for helping your students be successful."
"My sister who works in the neighboring school district says they are implementing blended learning. Don't you think we should do that?"	"That's good to know. When we review our data and make adjustments to our goals, strategies, and action steps we can consider how this might fit into our plan. Right now, however, our team spent lots of time developing a plan that is designed to meet the needs of our school. We don't want to put a new initiative into the plan until we see what impact our current plan has on student achievement."

Be an Active Participant

It goes without saying that coaches need to be on school improvement and/or leadership teams. Whatever the structure that the school has for developing the plan, coaches need to have a seat at the table. But beyond just being on the team, coaches need to take an active role. This doesn't mean that they take over and lead, although having teachers and coaches be cochairs is a good structure; it means that they contribute in ways that help the entire team get and stay focused. They do this by providing resources, asking difficult questions, and pointing the team back to the mission and student data. The effective questioning techniques that are a hallmark of student-centered coaching can be put to good use in these leadership team meetings. Since coaches get an upfront view of how students are performing across the school, they will have insights that many others will not. Pointing the team back to the benchmarks in the plan and discussing what this means for students is the duty of the coach.

Be a Connector

One of the most important roles the coach plays is to serve as a connector. It is easy for classroom teachers to lose sight of school improvement efforts given the day to day demands in the classroom. Coaches need to help teachers see the big picture by making the connection between classroom practice and the overall school goals. They do this by being keenly aware of what is in the plan, why it matters, and what impact it will have on students. During coaching cycles, coaches can focus questions around student outcomes identified in the plan and supported through professional development. For example, a coach may ask a teacher how what they learned about effective questioning made a difference on student learning in their classroom. They also do this by making sure that they steer clear of promoting practices that are counterproductive to the plan.

IN CLOSING

Schools are complex systems, so it is no surprise that leaders can lose their way when it comes to identifying and implementing reform efforts. Unwittingly we can find ourselves trying to juggle too many initiatives at once. We work tirelessly, and yet the needle on student achievement doesn't move. Breaking this cycle requires clarity and collaboration. It requires focus and follow-through. Connecting the processes for school improvement and understanding the coaches' role in these efforts helps make these things happen.

Building a house that stands the test of time requires clear plans and coordination. Leaders are wise to think in these same terms when it comes to improving their school. Principals coordinate the planning, design, and construction; coaches are the carpenters who build learning structures through their work with teachers. Working together in a coordinated fashion makes the hard work of improving student achievement a reality, not just for one student, but the entire school. Aligning school improvement processes, with a focus on clear plans, ensures that everyone in the system knows and understands his or her role in constructing lifelong learners.

3 Defining Roles for Coaches and Principals

"The winds and the waves are always on the side of the ablest navigators."

—Edward Gibbon

Growing up in coastal California, a tide calendar always hung on the wall of Diane's childhood kitchen. The tides were checked to avoid heading down to the beach when the waters were too high. On the beach you could always spot someone from out-of-town because they set up their things too close to the water's edge. As the tide came in, we would be high and dry, while their towels and shoes drifted out to sea. To us, the power of the tides was predictable. Yet it seemed to take many others by surprise. The key is anticipating the drift of the tides. The same goes for coaching. If we aren't on top of things (and if we don't clearly define the coach's role), then our coaching may also get washed out to sea.

There are many ways for the coach's role to be eroded. You may begin the school year feeling as if roles are solidly defined, only to find that other factors begin to interfere and chip away at that vision. Perhaps a coach is asked to manage assessment data, and pretty soon this seemingly small task has morphed into a part-time job. Maybe a coach chooses to focus on busy work rather than on engaging teachers in more robust coaching cycles. Teachers may begin to perceive the coach as a highly paid paraprofessional and may question whether it is a good use of resources. Slowly but surely, the coaching role changes. Just like the beachgoers shouldn't be surprised by the high tide, we shouldn't be surprised when this occurs.

WHY IT MATTERS

Vision + Duties + Responsibilities = Role

When discussing "roles," let's get clear about what we mean. It's a word that can be misunderstood, especially when we think of it as a discrete set of duties. This sells the notion short because it means we have failed to consider how one's role aligns with the broader vision for school improvement.

Rather than thinking about role purely as a set of duties, it can be helpful to focus on how it tucks into the broader vision for school improvement (Figure 3.1). Defining the coach's role in this way integrates the school vision, the coach's duties, and what the coach is responsible for achieving.

Figure 3.1 How We Define the Role of a Coach

Vision	Duties	Responsibilities
• The vision for school improvement • How the coach and principal will work together to implement the vision	• The duties that fill the coach's time • What's on the coach's calendar	• The responsibilities that are assigned to the coach • What the coach will be expected to achieve

As you read Figure 3.1, you'll notice an emphasis on alignment of the coach's role with the school improvement plan. This notion aligns with DuFour, Eaker, and DuFour's (2005) work on building professional learning communities when they write:

> In schools that progress as PLCs, staff members quickly move beyond mission statements to clarify the characteristics of the school they are trying to create in order to achieve their mission. They develop a shared vision of the school that is clear and compelling. Just as importantly, they identify the collective commitments each staff member must demonstrate if the school is to move toward its vision. These commitments are stated not as beliefs, but as specific behaviors or actions that clarify how individual staff members can contribute to the successful implementation of the vision. Finally, the staff identifies specific goals or indicators that

serve as benchmarks of their progress—targets and timelines that demand action if they are to be achieved. (pp. 229–230)

The fact is, we can't clearly define the role of the coach without establishing clarity around what we are trying to accomplish in the first place. This approach would be too generic and wouldn't account for the specific tasks that will be required to accomplish the vision for school improvement. Getting down to the brass tacks of duties and responsibilities is necessary if we hope to see the vision come to life.

As you read in Chapter 2, you learned about how to lead with a focused school improvement plan. This hard work pays off when it comes to defining the role of the coach because it is truly the first step in the process. Asking the question, "What are we trying to accomplish?" segues into a targeted conversation about the coach's role.

We also can't create a list of duties and expect that this will be enough. Taking this approach means we are thinking about the role of the coach in a vacuum. It sets us up for failure because the coach simply can't do it alone. Rather, we need to establish a solid principal and coach partnership that begins with the definition of how the two roles overlap. This involves a collaborative discussion wherein the principal and coach uncover how they will work together to implement the vision, the coach's duties, and what the coach will be responsible for accomplishing. Later in the chapter, we provide strategies for defining how the principal and coach will get clear about how their roles will overlap. Figure 3.2 provides an example of a clearly defined coaching role.

Figure 3.2 Defining the Principal and Coach Roles

Vision	Duties	Responsibilities
• Develop assessment-capable learners in all grades and subject areas. • The coach will provide support to teachers that is differentiated and includes choice for teachers. • The principal will define the expected instructional practices and hold teachers accountable for implementation.	• Facilitate coaching cycles. • Lead team planning sessions. • Work with the leadership team to co-plan professional learning. • Teach one advisory period. • Meet with the principal on a weekly basis. • Participate in district-level coaching training.	• Complete at least twelve coaching cycles across the school year. • Provide openings for coaching cycles every 6 weeks. • Document and share the impact of coaching cycles using the Results-Based Coaching Tool. • Deliver professional learning that engages adult learners.

We Are Happier When Our Roles Are Clearly Defined

Uncertainty regarding what others expect of us creates stress and unhappiness. When our role is clear, and we've made the choice that these duties are what we would like to engage in, then morale increases. When the reverse is true, and there is uncertainty around what is expected of us, our morale plummets. Simply put, we must be able to trust that we are "on the right seat on the bus." Otherwise, we feel topsy-turvy and unsure about whether we are doing a good job.

Denmark is known as the happiest country in the world. The Danes have held this top spot for years, and given the fact that this isn't likely due to the balmy weather, we thought we'd dig into this phenomenon. It turns out that the biggest factor that leads to happiness in Denmark is trust. Christian Bjørnskov, Professor at the Department of Economics and Business, at Aarhus University states, "In Denmark, we have an extremely high level of trust. That is one of the most important causes of our happiness" (Wiking, 2014). If you've ever worked in a school where trust was lacking, you may have experienced the stress that this creates. Imagine if this lack of trust applied to the duties that you were asked to do on a daily basis. Imagine if you couldn't really pin down how you fit into the broader plan for school improvement. You'd begin to distrust your very existence within the school. While this might sound alarmist, it manifests in small ways. A coach who feels lost and unsure may begin to dream of a new role in a new school. This is the drift that happens when we don't clearly define (and hold fast to) our roles.

Clarity of role also hinges on understanding what we are there to accomplish in the first place. Harvard Business School has researched the link between happiness and the workplace. They found that understanding our progress was critical. In other words, we are happier when we understand how our work is making a difference. Amabile and Kramer (2011) write, "As long as workers experience their labor as meaningful, progress is often followed by joy and excitement about the work" (p. 65). Without clearly defined roles, this feeling will be out of reach. With clearly defined roles, coaches are more likely to see their work as meaningful and thus understand the day-to-day progress that is being made.

Roles and Beliefs Go Hand-in-Hand

It's important to remember that when we discuss roles, we ought to consider our beliefs as well. The two go hand-in-hand because they comprise the operating system by which we live our lives. A school leader can do a bang-up job defining the role of the coach, but if it doesn't match the coach's beliefs, then it is likely that the plan will never come to fruition. The primary reason for this is a lack of motivation due to a lack of clear purpose. In the bestselling book, *Drive*, Daniel Pink (2009) summarizes an interview with psychologist Mihaly Csikszentmihalyi, who said, "Purpose provides activation energy for living" (p. 132). We need coaches to feel activated so that they'll dig into the complex and challenging work that lies before them. For this to occur, beliefs and purpose must be taken into account.

Consider a school that just adopted a new literacy curriculum, and the expectation is for the coach to ensure that the program is implemented with fidelity. Seems pretty straightforward until we layer in the fact that the coach believed in taking a student-centered approach. This very conundrum was faced by a coach whom we have worked with over the past several years. When Samuel became a literacy coach, he was asked to take a student-centered approach. This matched his beliefs, and he was having a lot of success building partnerships throughout his school. With the new adoption came the expectation that he would be checking to see if people were implementing the new literacy program. This made Samuel uncomfortable. To make things worse, he didn't agree with how the program approached literacy instruction. So here he was, holding people accountable for something he didn't believe in. This put Samuel in a position where his beliefs were no longer in alignment with his role.

So what were his options? Samuel might choose to set his beliefs aside and follow through as expected by the principal. The problem with this approach is that his heart wouldn't be in it and he would be far less effective as a coach. This is not a sustainable option. He might be able to do it for a little while, but he will most likely end up in a new role in the future due to the disconnect he would be living on a daily basis.

Another option is he could hold true to his beliefs about coaching and literacy instruction. The obvious problem with this approach is he would be going head to head with the vision that was set forth by the district. This would create a lack of focus and probable confusion among teachers. Again, not a sustainable option.

The best approach is for Samuel and his principal to discuss their beliefs *before* they plan what coaching will look like with the new adoption. In this way, they would be more likely to be on the same page. Seeking common ground in this way would help integrate Samuel into the adoption in a way that bridges the district vision and his belief system. For example, they may decide that he will lead professional learning sessions around how to use the program, while still doing coaching cycles that take a more student-centered approach. Or maybe the principal will commit to holding the teachers accountable for implementing the new curriculum and taking that off Samuel's plate. Another option would be for Samuel to be provided with additional training regarding how the program works so that he isn't making assumptions based on an incomplete vision. Or perhaps he can find ways to subtly tweak his coaching cycles without losing his vision for what good coaching looks like.

What's most important is that the principal and coach work through their vision and how it will be adjusted to meet the current reality. Figure 3.3 provides a list of questions that can guide these conversations. If there are dramatic differences in viewpoint, then this is a signal to slow down and work through any differences, before plowing ahead.

Figure 3.3   Framing Our Beliefs Around Teaching and Learning

1. How do we believe that adults learn best?

2. What are our beliefs regarding how students learn best?

3. What do we think effective coaching looks like?

4. How can coaches use their time most effectively?

5. What do we believe are the most effective practices for teaching (math, literacy, etc.)?

6. How will we use curriculum and resources to support student achievement in our school?

7. What do we believe are the necessary steps for holding teachers accountable? What are our roles in this?

WHAT IT LOOKS LIKE

Clarifying how the role of the principal and coach will overlap is an essential step for any coaching program. We simply can't make assumptions about this because there are far too many considerations related to coaching and evaluation to leave it up to chance.

Leadership Move #1: Understand How the Role of the Principal and Coach Overlaps

We use a Venn diagram to frame this conversation because it is a familiar process that reminds us to think about what will be unique to each role and what will be shared. As you review the Venn diagram (Figure 3.4), you'll notice that there are clear differences based on the fact that the principal is the supervisor (and evaluator) of teachers and the coach is there to provide support. We discuss this notion of separating coaching from supervision further in Chapter 7. For now, we ask that you set aside time to engage in this conversation with your coach. In this way you will both understand your roles and how they work together.

Leadership Move #2: Attend to All the Roles Within a District

There are many roles in a school system. The school board sets policy and is often responsible for making a coaching program possible. Most school boards expect information regarding the ongoing impact of this investment. The superintendent guides the board vision. District leaders support implementation, lead decision making on curriculum and resources, and provide professional development. The principal leads the effort with a specific focus on his or her own student and teacher population. The coach provides student-centered support by building partnerships throughout the school. Teachers are on the front lines ensuring that students are learning. And students do the learning.

Figure 3.4 Comparing Principal and Coach Roles

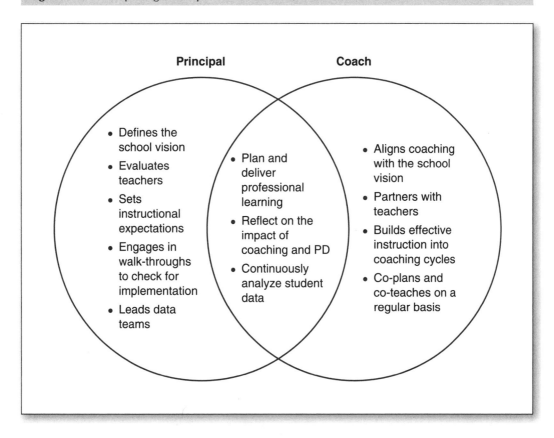

In the book *Coaching Matters*, the authors speak to these key players within the district (Killion, Harrison, Bryan, & Clifton, 2012). Each of these stakeholders is essential to ensure that the coaching effort is clearly defined and well implemented. If any are left out of the conversation, then mixed messages and confusion will likely occur.

The simple move of informing and seeking feedback from these constituencies is not to be underestimated. This may take the form of biannual board updates about the impact coaching is making on teaching and learning. Superintendents and other district leaders may be expected to attend and learn alongside coaches on a regular basis to provide them with a clear vision of what student-centered coaching looks like in practice. Teachers may be asked for feedback regarding how coaching is impacting their classrooms. District leaders who coordinate coaching must be supported. This is a demanding job given the complexity of coaching. If the people who are supporting coaches aren't supported, then we are in trouble.

Leadership Move #3: Beware of the Quasi-Administrator

A common misstep regarding roles is what we refer to as the *quasi-administrator*. This occurs when the coach serves in an administrative capacity. It may show up subtly with the coach taking on duties that are in the arena of supervision, such as being the point person for teachers to turn in minutes from collaboration meetings such as PLCs, following up with teachers to be sure they get their data in on time, or putting the coach in the role of facilitating data teams. Coaches may also be viewed as quasi-administrators based on the committees they serve on, or even where their office is located. If it's next door to the principal's office, a space usually dedicated to the assistant principal, then it might suggest that the coach is taking on an administrative role. Another common scenario is the principal who inherits a coach who takes on the stance of an administrator. If these behaviors aren't nipped in the bud quickly, then it will not only erode the principal's authority, but it will erode the coaching program as well.

Using the coach as a quasi-administrator may occur if the school leader feels under pressure to get results quickly and sees teacher development through the lens of compliance. Boiling down school improvement to "if we make them do it, then everything will be okay" fails to acknowledge the complexity of what we are after. Trusting the process of coaching is essential if we are going to "lead" the process. Asking the coach to serve as another administrator isn't going to get us there. Instead, clearing the decks and allowing a coach to build capacity is what we are after.

Sometimes coaches take on these duties because they'd rather be the boss than serve as a coach. In these cases, coaches will struggle to build trusting relationships with teachers because nobody will be sure where they stand. This will lead to a lack of trust and some degree of confusion. The fact is, being a learner requires vulnerability and if folks are on guard, then learning will be diminished.

Understanding if coaches see themselves as a quasi-administrator is a matter of asking why they have chosen to be a coach in the first place. If the answer falls into the territory of "making people do things," then it would be a good idea to be wary because there is no faster way to muddy the waters than a coach taking on an administrative role. We recommend clear separation between coaching and supervision so that everyone knows where they stand. More on this in Chapter 7.

Leadership Move #4: Broadly Communicate the Coach's Role

Student-centered coaching requires a principal who understands the rationale and practices for this type of coaching and then articulates with confidence how coaching will positively impact student learning. This process of articulation hinges on creating a plan for defining what student-centered coaching means for the teachers and students. Consider this as an opportunity to build buzz and excitement about coaching.

Being savvy regarding this messaging may feel like the principal is being asked to act like a cheerleader for coaching, and that is okay. One of the primary roles of the leader is to be an advocate for kids, and student-centered coaching is all about helping kids. It's a whole lot like marketing of a product. Teachers have to believe in coaching, and if they sense even the smallest lack of support by the principal, then they will take that as an excuse to remain on the sidelines. The following steps walk you through how to build excitement around coaching. These are presented in an intentional order because starting with the "why" is how we begin to win the hearts and minds of teachers. More on this in Chapter 5.

1. **Define why coaching matters.** *Articulate why teachers should care.*

2. **Communicate how coaching aligns with other district initiatives.** *Make sure teachers understand that coaching isn't one more thing.*

3. **Share the coach's role and how it folds into the plan for school improvement.** *Help teachers see the coach as inherent to the school's success.*

4. **Describe the expectations for teacher participation in coaching.** *Identify what participation looks like and how much time it will take.*

5. **Outline how teachers will be provided with choice and ownership in the coaching process.** *Make coaching about more than compliance.*

Leadership Move #5: Create Systems to Protect the Coach's Role

In the article, *Pave the Way for Coaches*, Heineke and Polnick (2013) discuss the importance of ensuring that most of a coach's time is spent coaching. They write,

> The top priority of instructional coaches should be to facilitate teacher learning that will translate into greater student learning. When the focus of instructional coaching is fractured, meeting professional learning goals becomes doubtful, so clearly defining the coaching role and supporting that work is a necessary first step. (p. 50)

One of our favorite systems for protecting the coach's role is regular calendar reviews with the principal. The ideal time for this to occur is every 4 to 6 weeks. This helps coaches craft a new calendar as they launch a new round of coaching cycles. Checking in at the beginning of the new round provides the principal with the opportunity to make sure that the coach is mostly in coaching cycles. It's also a way to help the coach achieve balance between duties that are coaching related and duties that might be for another purpose.

It's also important to anticipate and create a plan for the inevitable things that will draw a coach away from coaching. A common example is subbing in classrooms. Creating a system to address it is an important step that can be taken by the school leader.

Susan, a principal of a rural K–12 school, faced this challenge due to a substitute shortage in her district. Whenever a classroom needed to be covered, the secretary picked up the phone and called the coach. Out of fear of disappointing, the coach always agreed. With time, the coach's role become so eroded that she no longer felt she could arrange coaching cycles because she was pulled out so often.

Susan decided to intervene at the front line: the secretary. She created a list of all certified staff in the school who didn't have a dedicated class. This included the coach, ESL teacher, librarian, psychologist, and social worker. Susan then provided the secretary with a checklist to rotate through who would provide coverage each time it was required (Figure 3.5). The checklist provided a structure for the front office and also served as a simple tool for collecting data. At the end of each month, Susan reviewed the data to make sure that the system was still working.

LESSON FROM THE FIELD

Nido de Aguilas is a PreK–12 international school in the foothills of the Andes near Santiago, Chile. Over the last 3 years, the school has embarked on a vision of professional learning known as, "Nido Learns Together."

Figure 3.5 Front Office Checklist for Assigning Coverage

Checklist for Assigning Coverage				
Month (circle) Aug Sept Oct Nov Dec Jan Feb Mar April May June				
Use the following rotation when assigning coverage. Only skip if the person identified is absent.				
	Date	**Date**	**Date**	**Date**
Jennifer, Coach Extension, 4235				
Marelena, ESL Extension, 4992				
Becca, Librarian Extension, 4011				
Maggie, Psychologist Extension, 4776				
Peter, Social Worker Extension, 4449				

The emphasis was on developing a collaborative environment that supports teachers at all levels of experience. Around the same time, the school hired two coaches who served under the title of specialist. Soon thereafter, two more coaches were hired, and the school officially launched the coaching program.

Rather than jumping into implementation, they began with a prelaunch phase so that the leadership team and coaches could work together to define what coaching would look like at their school. This was a 6-month-long process that led to a clear articulation of the vision and roles for coaching.

During the prelaunch phase, they spent time getting smarter about coaching. Diane visited the school to work with the administrators, coaches, and teachers. This included preparing a vision for coaching cycles, planning how to communicate this to teachers, and building trust throughout the school.

These messages were communicated among all staff members so that there would be no confusion about the purpose for coaching. One such meeting included Diane sharing background and beliefs for student-centered coaching. She emphasized that it's about partnering to support student learning and promised that the coaches would never approach coaching through a deficit lens. In other words, they wouldn't be running around looking for teachers' flaws and bossing them around. The teachers then asked questions about how coaching would impact them, what they would be expected to do, and anything else that was on their minds.

As a follow up, the principal and assistant principal met with each team to discuss what coaching is and what coaching isn't. These conversations were personalized and specific to the individuals. Teachers asked questions such as "Will this tie to my evaluation?" and "Do I have to participate?" It was made clear that the school administrators would handle all evaluation matters and that the coaches would work on an opt-in basis. Almost 3 years later, 92% of teachers have participated in at least one coaching cycle and 69% have participated in even more.

As soon as a foundation was laid, the coaches were ready for the launch phase. This included offering mini coaching cycles so that the teachers could get a taste of student-centered coaching. Creating this opportunity reinforced the fact that coaching was student-centered and that it would focus on supported teachers to meet their goals for students.

A clear and articulated vision went a long way in getting coaching off on the right foot. It also led to more robust partnerships that were built on trust because everyone was on the same page. Nothing was left to chance, and coaching is thriving at Nido.

WHERE ARE YOU NOW?

Clearly defining (and sticking with) the coach's role requires both tenacity and focus. It is easy for the role to become diluted when we lose sight of how coaching moves learning forward in the school. The following assessment is designed to help school leaders stay true to their vision for coaching (Figure 3.6).

Troubleshooting Around Implementation of Student-Centered Coaching

Inevitably, a principal will face difficult decisions around how to allocate existing resources within a sea of demands. Most likely, the coach will be one of the first staff members who gets pulled into extraneous duties. The following conversations starters will guide the principal through some common ways that a coach might be pulled away from his or her role (Figure 3.7).

THE COACH'S ROLE

It's not just the principal's job to advocate for, and protect, the coaching role. A fair amount of the responsibility rests on the shoulders of the

Figure 3.6 Self-Assessment for School Leaders

Clearly Define the Coach's Role			
	Accomplished	**Developing**	**Novice**
The School Leader	Works with the coach to define what coaching is about. The coach's role is then publicized to the broader school community. It is also revisited throughout the year to encourage teacher participation and reinforce how the coach is positioned to impact student and teacher learning.	Attempts to define the role of the coach, but there may be things on the coach's list of duties that pull them away from coaching. Or as the year progresses, the role of the coach isn't maintained. Teachers have an uneven vision of the coach's role, or why there is even a coach in the school.	Defers to others to define the coach's role. Others may be district leadership, the coach, or fate. The coach's role isn't publicized, and teachers do not have a shared vision of why there is a coach in the school.
Success Criteria	I can . . . • Reflect with my coach using a Venn diagram to determine how the principal and coach role overlaps and is distinct. • Guard the coach's role and responsibilities. • Support the coach to build systems and structures that align with their role. • Work with the coach to develop a communications plan to publicize the coach's role. • Continually reinforce the importance of coaching as well as the role of the coach. • Delegate busy work to other staff members.		

Figure 3.7 Language for Defining the Coach's Role

If I hear . . .	Then I can say . . .
"We are short substitutes again. Can the coach cover a class?"	"We have a system for providing coverage. This way we won't continuously pull the coach from existing coaching duties. I understand that providing coverage is an inconvenience. This is why we spread it out across the staff members who don't teach in a regular classroom."
[The principal's supervisor says], "We need that data by Friday. Your coach can do this."	"Our coach's schedule is mostly comprised of working with teachers in their classrooms and during planning conversations. If they cancel on teachers, then student learning will be impacted. We'll work on putting that data together, but since we don't have a dedicated 'data person' it might take a bit longer than expected."
"The coach seems to have a lot of flexibility. Couldn't we use that position to lower our class sizes?"	"The coach's time does look different than a classroom teacher's time. It's important to understand that the coach is being held accountable for increasing student achievement and supporting teacher development just like any teacher. Coaching is very important for our school. Without a coach, we would have a much harder time reaching our goals."

coach as well. This can be overwhelming for many coaches. They leave the classroom, where they are provided a bell schedule and classes that they are expected to teach, to a coaching role that is generally undefined and open ended.

Coaches who are able to create a system and schedule for their work typically get further because they are able to figure out what their day-to-day work will look like. Coaches who struggle to create systems will find themselves floating and unsure of how they should be spending their time. This never feels good. We recommend for coaches to take the following steps to solidify their role.

Schedule Coaching Cycles

When a coach's role is poorly defined, anything goes. And when anything goes, it is hard to get traction with coaching cycles. We suggest that coaches get very concrete with their schedules, not just for themselves but for others as well. Figure 3.8 provides an example of how a middle school coach carved out time for coaching, even though she was tasked with many other duties.

Beth is a middle school coach who is also responsible for teaching a math class and advisory. This schedule is for a 6-week period of time. As you review the schedule, you'll notice that she is currently engaged in three coaching cycles. Two of the cycles are with individual teachers (Joe and Chelsea). The other cycle is with the 8th-grade language arts team. Beth has dedicated time for weekly co-planning as well as time in each teacher's classroom. This is what we are looking for when we suggest that coaches need to develop a schedule that is focused on the right things: coaching cycles. At the end of this round, Beth will change her schedule so that she can work with a different group of teachers.

While this example isn't color coded, we find that using colors helps the coach and principal find patterns in how time is being allocating to coaching. For example, if a coach is spending most of the week in grade level meetings, then this trend will be more obvious. We advocate for most of a coach's schedule to indicate two things: co-teaching in classrooms and co-planning. These are the most important aspects of student-centered coaching, and that's where we want to see a coach's time spent. When working with teams of coaches, we recommend that they color code their schedule using the following key.

- Yellow: Planning time for the coach
- Purple: Co-planning with teachers
- Red: Co-teaching in classrooms

Figure 3.8 Sample Schedule for Middle School Coaching Cycles

	Monday	Tuesday	Wednesday	Thursday	Friday
7:30–8:00	Advisory With 8th Graders				
8:00–9:00	Teach Pre-Algebra				
9:10–10:10	Coaching Meeting at District	Joe: Co-Teaching (6th-grade math)	Joe: Co-Teaching (6th-grade math)	Joe: Co-Teaching (6th-grade math)	Chelsea: Co-Planning (7th-grade social studies)
10:20–11:30		Chelsea: Co-Teaching (7th-grade social studies)	Chelsea: Co-Teaching (7th-grade social studies)	8th-Grade LA Team: Weekly Co-Planning	Weekly Meeting With the Principal
11:30–12:00	Lunch				
12:10–1:00	Informal Coaching With Teachers				
1:10–2:00	Joe: Co-Planning (6th-grade math)	8th-Grade LA Team: Co-Teaching With Sarah	8th-Grade LA Team: Co-Teaching With Shelly	8th-Grade LA Team: Co-Teaching With Mike	Curriculum Team Meeting
2:10–3:00	Prep for Coaching and Pre-Algebra				

Source: Sweeney, D. (2011). *Student-Centered Coaching: A Guide for K–8 Principals and Coaches.* Used with permission.

- Orange: Time spent in PLCs or other collaboration time
- Blue: Standing meetings with principal and district
- Gray: Other duties
- Purple: Informal support/providing resources

Coaches can then analyze their schedules to pinpoint how they are using their time and what tweaks they might make. As we suggested earlier in this chapter, we also recommend for the coach's schedule to be reviewed during principal and coach meetings. If nobody is keeping an eye on the coach's time, then it may be slipping out to sea.

Make Your Schedule Public

The easiest way to make a coaching schedule public is to hang it on the door of the coach's office. This sends a strong message that the coach is fully engaged in important work. It also provides a degree of predictability and counteracts the randomness that some coaches feel. It's also much harder to pull a coach from coaching duties if the time is allocated to something important. This is another reason that we suggest creating a schedule that lasts a whole round of coaching cycles (4–6 weeks) rather than scheduling on a week-to-week or day-to-day basis. We call week-to-week scheduling "scheduling like a dentist." It occurs when we pull out our calendar and schedule meetings one at a time. This structure approach doesn't provide the structure we are looking for. It also becomes more challenging to make your schedule public because it is changing all the time.

We suggest scheduling like a physical therapist. This implies that reaching the goal is going to take some time, so we arrange a series of connected conversations across 4 weeks to 6 weeks that include planning sessions and co-teaching. Taking this approach allows coaches to build (and share) a predictable schedule that will set them up to reach their goals for teacher and student learning.

IN CLOSING

We all deserve a clearly defined role. With this type of clarity, we wake up every day understanding what we are there to accomplish. Without it, we are adrift and unsure of how we fit into the bigger picture. The sad truth is that it isn't uncommon for coaches to be hired and nobody's quite sure about their role. That's a hard space to occupy for very long.

This chapter has provided some concrete things that a principal and coach can do to define the coach's role. But underneath all those nitty-gritty tasks lies our hopes and dreams for students. If we can carve out a clear role, then we can envision how we can make a difference. We must take care of that dream and not allow it to be eroded with busy work that takes us away from what's important. This brings to mind the poem *Dreams*, by Langston Hughes. He reminds us that we must "hold fast" to our dreams. Coaching matters, and it's important work. So let's hold fast to that dream and make it a reality.

4 School Culture and Coaching

"There can be no significant learning, without significant relationships."

—James Comer

Any parent knows that while having a child is a joyful experience, it also causes a certain amount of disequilibrium in the household. The level of disruption can depend on how much time and thought the parents have put into planning for an additional person in their lives. Astute parents understand that things will need to work differently, and then plan according. The same mindset is needed by principals when integrating coaches into a school culture. Adding the unique role of coaches into a school setting will change the dynamics in the school community. Whether or not this will be a positive or negative change rests solely on the shoulders of the principal. Figuring out how to ensure that the shift is positive is job number one.

Key to determining the coach's impact is understanding that the school climate is a reflection of the norms, values, and interpersonal relationships of *all* individuals in the school. Just as a new baby won't fix a marriage in trouble, coaches aren't the panacea for improving the school's culture. Infusing coaches into a school can provide a much needed restart to examine the rituals and behaviors in the school, but culture is bigger than how the coach works with teachers and the principal. These relationships contribute to the school climate, but aren't the driver. Having a healthy relationship with the coach isn't enough to ensure that the entire school culture will be positive. The purpose of this chapter isn't to tell you how to create a positive culture in your school. There are many excellent

● 57

books on that topic that you can read. The purpose is to provide leaders with strategies to integrate coaches so they can contribute to an overall positive school culture.

WHY IT MATTERS

Keep the Main Thing the Main Thing

Seeing the reciprocal relationship that culture, teaching, and learning play in schools can be challenging. This lack of clarity can lead to misconceptions about how to address culture. The thinking goes something like this, *"First*, we need to build relationships of trust with the staff, and *then* we can get to implementing reforms." Or *"First* we need to improve culture, and *then* we can work improving instruction." These things can't be separated because culture informs instruction, and instruction informs culture. They go hand in hand.

Viviane Robinson (2011) says it best,

> Effective educational leadership is not about getting the relationships right and then tackling the difficult work challenges. It is about doing both simultaneously so that the relationships are strengthened through doing the hard, collective work of improving teaching and learning. (p. 16)

Developing a positive culture, regardless of whether there are coaches or not in the school, requires the principal to focus efforts on teaching and learning. This is the first step in ensuring that coaches will have a positive impact.

Integrating coaches into a culture where learning is a priority increases their effectiveness because everyone is speaking a similar language. Consider how different the transition to student-centered coaching would be in a school where learning targets and formative assessments are just the way they do business, versus a school where professional learning communities (PLCs) are seen as optional and teachers teach from the textbook. When learning is front and center, coaches are welcomed as another support in the pursuit of student learning. They can jump right in to help teachers meet their goals. When this isn't the case, coaches are seen as a threat and treated with mistrust and suspicion. Culture is not simply an action; it is an outcome of intentional actions taken within the system (Mausbach & Morrison, 2016). Principals who intentionally put learning first set up coaches and ultimately students for success.

Inclusive Environments Require Collaboration

If an inclusive school environment for all students regardless of race, religion, gender, or sexual orientation is what is desired, this requires more than dialogue. It requires the hands-on, side-by-side deep learning that occurs when principals, coaches, and teachers work together to ferret out the thorny issues associated with teaching students with diverse needs.

Teachers' beliefs or misconceptions about student learning won't change by leaders simply telling them something is the right thing to do. Teachers need to be supported to practice new approaches so their thinking and ultimately their beliefs shift. Changing behavior helps change thinking (Sinek, 2015). Coaches play a critical role in this process because, and if allowed, they create a safe space where teachers can feel comfortable to share, learn, grow, and even stumble now and again. Effective collaboration requires a dose of vulnerability, and this is difficult to do without the type of support coaches provide.

Trust Matters

The issue of trust surfaces in every leadership book because it is such a powerful indicator of the health of the organization. Trust is critical because it sets the tone for how the organization will function. In schools, the level of trust determines not only how staff will work together, but also impacts both the social and academic progress of students (Bryk & Schneider, 2002; Tschannen-Moran & Hoy, 2000). Trust can't be demanded by a school leader, but rather is earned through day-to-day actions. According to Kirtman and Fullan (2016), ". . . trust and action go hand in hand" (p. 20). Building a high trust school where teachers have a strong sense of professional community and are willing to take risks requires a leader who is clear and consistent in actions and deeds.

When coaches are introduced in a school, the issue of trust surfaces right away. Ann vividly remembers a group of new coaches telling her that teachers in the district felt that coaches were hired to fire bad teachers. How would these coaches make headway when so much trust was lacking?

This reminds us that assigning a coach to a school and ignoring the trust factor is a less than strategic approach. Getting a clear sense of how teachers view coaching helps the principal determine how much trust building is required. Being clear about what coaches will and won't do helps counter mistrust and fear. The process is continuous. After coaches are deployed, the principal must continue to build trust through monitoring teaching and learning and helping support the coach to fulfill the role.

WHAT IT LOOKS LIKE

Building a positive culture around coaching requires more from the building leader than simply having a pulse on the school climate. Modeling a growth mindset, making learning transparent, taking risks as a learner, and listening are fundamental practices for leaders who desire a culture where learning is front and center. The moves outlined below will help principals become more adept at these behaviors, ensuring that the school becomes a place where everyone (student, teacher, coach) comes wanting to learn.

Leadership Move #1: Quit Playing "Whack a Mole"

Leading a school can sometimes feel like a game of whack a mole where things pop up unexpectedly. This diverts the leader's attention. Breaking out of this vicious cycle requires a leader to be clear about the work he or she needs to commit to that will make a difference for students. But with so much going on in a school, it can be difficult to make and keep commitments. Even when a principal has good intentions, coaches can end up leading instruction for the entire school because the principal is mired in management issues. Focusing on three core commitments can help move leaders into a more proactive stance (Mausbach & Morrison, 2016).

Figure 4.1 outlines three leadership commitments and provides examples of how coaches help leaders maintain this focus. The commitments drive consistency because they frame leader's actions. They help the leader put down the mallet and stop "chasing the mole" so they can instead look up and model being the lead learner. Commitments also help the coaches work in partnership with the principal so they can "stay in their lane" and help the school stay on course. A sure fire way to erode school culture is to have everyone in the school feel like they are in a frenzy. Upholding these commitments is the antidote to that.

Leadership Move #2: Build Collective Efficacy by Letting Coaches Do Their Job

Learning flourishes in an environment where people (both adults and students) believe they have what it takes to be successful. This is why collective teacher efficacy is such a powerful influence on student achievement, with a 1.57 effect size. Considering that a .40 effect size equals a year's worth of growth, collective efficacy has the potential to quadruple the rate of student learning (Donohoo, 2017; Hattie, 2015). The

Figure 4.1 Leadership Commitments

Commitment	How Principals Lead the Commitment	How Coaches Positively Contribute Support
Promoting a safe culture	• Value teachers' time by using whole group gatherings for learning. • Share weekly schedule for observing and sitting in on collaboration (i.e., PLCs) so everyone in the school is aware that these times are interruption free.	• Use student-centered coaching moves during coaching cycles. • Serve as a team member, not a team leader for collaboration (i.e., PLCs). • Keep coaching commitments.
Implementation of school improvement processes at high levels	• Schedule weekly observations the week prior rather than trying to randomly get into classrooms each day. • Use the mission and vision as a lens for decision making.	• Participate on school leadership team. • Provide honest and open feedback to principal regarding the plan's progress or lack thereof.
Using a growth mindset to enhance professional capital	• Develop a schedule for weekly collaboration meetings and attend religiously. • Set aside time to meet weekly with the coach.	• Use student-centered coaching moves during coaching cycles. • Meet weekly with the principal.

challenge for school leaders is to create opportunities for teachers to feel and be successful. One of the most powerful ways they can do this is by letting coaches do their work. Student-centered coaching is designed to increase collective efficacy because it is all about helping teachers reach their goals for student learning. When coaching is geared around student outcomes, then we are not only improving instruction in the moment, but we also are creating conditions for student success. This directly impacts the school culture.

Figure 4.2 outlines how student-centered coaching (Sweeney & Harris, 2016) impacts collective teacher efficacy by promoting the four major sources that contribute to self-efficacy beliefs: mastery experiences, vicarious experiences, social and verbal persuasion, and a positive emotional state (Bandura, 1997; Bloomberg & Pitchford, 2017; Donohoo, 2017). Simply put, increasing self-efficacy is at the heart of student-centered coaching. (For more information on these coaching moves, please read Appendix D.)

Figure 4.2 Alignment of Sources of Efficacy to Student-Centered Coaching Moves

Source	Student-Centered Coaching Moves
Mastery Experiences Opportunities to feel success	Setting Goals for Coaching Cycles Measuring the Impact of Coaching Co-Teaching Lessons Providing Strengths-Based Feedback
Vicarious Experiences Opportunities to observe others who are successful (models of success)	Using Learning Targets Micro Modeling Thinking Aloud About Instructional Decision Making Participating in Student-Centered Learning Labs
Social and Verbal Persuasion Communication is given about performance, includes feedback	Providing Strengths-Based Feedback Sorting Student Work Listening Asking Open-Ended Questions
Positive Emotional State Feeling safe to learn and take risks	Getting Ready for Coaching in the Classroom, or Setting Norms With Teachers Before Coaching Noticing and Naming Celebrating Student Growth

Understanding the impact collective teacher efficacy has on student achievement means that it just makes sense for principals to provide coaches with the time they need to do this work. Principals have to advocate for, and protect, coaches' time so they can dig in and use these moves. Tending to the coach's learning is also critical because it helps ensure that these moves have the desired impact. More on supporting the development of coaches in Chapter 8.

Leadership Move #3: Avoid Having Coaches Do All the Heavy Lifting for Teams

One marker of a happy relationship is how couples treat each other. The same can be said for schools. A marker of a healthy culture is how teams treat each other. A healthy culture requires teams that work effectively. Just as having one person do all the housework is a recipe for disaster, so is having coaches carry the weight of the team by doing all the facilitating and directing learning. This practice nurtures complacency in teachers and resentment in coaches. Coaches need to be active participants, but capacity building will be hindered if coaches are *always* in the leadership role.

While we don't want coaches to take over team collaboration, we also don't want them to leave teachers to figure it out all on their own. We have recently encountered a dynamic where teams aren't engaging in student-centered planning. Rather, they are dividing up the work and then sharing their plans with one another. While we understand the desire to be efficient, this habit is detrimental to the school culture because it short-circuits reflection and student-centered instruction.

Diane recently met with a group of principals and got an earful about this practice. One principal complained, "They make it clear that they don't want me in there during team meetings." Another said, "I know, I'm struggling to get them to plan their lessons collaboratively." As Diane listened, she was pulled in two directions. She understood the pressure teachers are under to teach new curriculum. Of course they want to be efficient. But she worried that they weren't using their planning time to be responsive to their students' needs. That's when a principal spoke up and said, "Our teachers don't do that anymore." The group turned and asked in unison, "How'd you do that?" She laughed and said, "I told them they couldn't. It's not the way we do things in our school." It's an answer that is so easy, yet so challenging.

We have to make the most of collaborative planning. If we don't, then why are teachers planning together in the first place? We can't take over planning agendas because this shuts down inquiry and ownership by teachers. It may also feel like decisions have been predetermined and that their voice isn't being heard. Yet the coach can't take a hands-off attitude either. Otherwise, we may end up with ineffective collaboration strategies.

Rich learning occurs when teachers, coaches, and principals have multiple opportunities to examine the impact of instructional practices, question their efficiency, discuss implications, and adjust thinking. A culture of collaborative inquiry provides the platform for this work. *Collaborative* being the key word here. Collaborative inquiry requires teachers to come together to identify professional dilemmas and determine solutions through inquiry, problem solving, and reflection (Donohoo, 2017). Solving tough teaching and learning issues requires everyone at the table to have an equal voice. Rotating the team leader role is one way to make this happen. Having a common template for team agendas, using protocols to examine student work, and making and checking in on team norms help teams function properly and keep the coach as a participant rather than always being the team leader.

Leadership Move #4: Embrace the Coach

It's difficult to underestimate the importance of the relationship between the principal and coach, and because of this we address aspects of developing and nurturing this relationship throughout this book. Without a healthy relationship between the principal and the coach it is impossible to have a healthy school culture. Just as the captain of a ship needs a first and second mate to keep the ship afloat, principals need coaches to help them navigate the choppy waters of school improvement. The coach's proximity to the real work in classrooms provides them with a unique perspective that principals need to ensure that they are on course and that the crew isn't contemplating mutiny. Leaders nurture this relationship by being real with coaches. A relationship of trust is built when the principal is vulnerable, letting coaches in by sharing that they need their help to solve issues in the school. A principal we've worked with said she sometimes opens her weekly coaches meeting by saying, "Help!" Nurturing a strong relationship with the coach requires authenticity, vulnerability, and at times a bit of uncomfortableness. Leaders need to let the coaches in so that what comes out of this relationship are powerful solutions to moving the school forward.

Leadership Move #5: Recognize and Address Conflict

Mechanics understand and expect that sometimes the parts in a car won't work properly so they need to take a good long look under the hood. Principals need this same mentality when it comes to conflict in their school. Avoiding conflict has the same disastrous effect as ignoring the flashing check engine light. The adults in schools will at times experience difficulty working together. This is inevitable. How the leader addresses conflict is what determines whether the school will run smoothly.

When conflict avoidance is the norm in a school it creates a vacuum that coaches may find themselves getting sucked into for the sake of creating harmony. While well intended, this behavior undermines the culture of the school because it moves the coach away from the core mission of being student-centered. Coaches will begin to be seen as fixers rather than partners. Leaders have to figure out how to address conflict in such a way that leads to growth. Three time nominee for the Nobel Peace Prize, Scilla Elworthy, sums it up this way, "Buried under the dragon's foot is a gem— something to be learned from conflict. And so you have to be able to name what is going on—and then talk about it in a way that isn't explosive" (Heffernan, 2015).

Transforming conflict into something productive requires leaders to make the most mistakes. Developing a culture where mistakes are shared not only helps others learn, but also communicates that mistakes are part of the learning process. Think of how transformed a culture would be if team meetings opened with, "This is what I did this week that didn't go well, can you help me identify why?" Critical questions such as, "Why is this important?", "Who does this decision affect?", and "How does this help us meet our mission?" are also important in addressing conflict. Rich debates require leaders to use questions to help unearth underlying issues and frustrations that may be standing in the way of progress. A corner-stone of student-centered coaching is being able to have deep authentic conversations about student learning. This is impossible in an environment where conflicts get buried or avoided.

Coaches can also inadvertently create or elevate conflict when they feel it is their job to get teachers to toe the line when it comes to implementing new initiatives or monitoring the school improvement plan. Besides being clear about roles and responsibilities, leaders address this by making sure that monitoring is central to their daily work. Coaches are not the implementation police, and the only way to ensure that they don't become this is for the principal to be in classrooms on a daily basis monitoring teaching and learning. Handing off instructional leadership duties will inherently create conflict because it puts coaches in a role that they were neither hired for, nor trained to do. Having a coach doesn't mean that principals spend less time on teaching and learning; what it means is that the principal has a partner in the school to help them navigate student learning issues.

LESSON FROM THE FIELD

Kim, the leader of a large middle school, was grateful for the relationship she had developed with her leadership team, even though at times it wasn't always easy to hear what they had to say. The team, which consisted of three coaches, department heads, and teachers, provided rich reflection on the important teaching and learning issues in the school. At the end of the previous school year, the teachers had shared that they felt they needed to take a bigger role in leading professional learning teams. As much as they appreciated having an administrator on these teams, they felt they were too top down and that the leaders rather than teachers were driving these meetings.

Kim was excited about teachers wanting more ownership over the PLCs and was appreciative that her leadership team felt they could openly share their views on the current situation. Over the summer they met and discussed how to reboot learning teams so their focus would be on using learning targets, which was a central strategy in the school's improvement plan. They decided that the teachers on the leadership team would become PLC team leaders.

As the school year got underway and team meetings were taking shape, Kim kept her pulse on the culture of the school by conducting her usual walk-throughs and attending PLC meetings. She also met weekly with the coaches as a group and individually. She sensed that the PLC leaders were overwhelmed, but wasn't sure if it was due to their new roles or to changes in the schedule. When she asked them for feedback they commented that they were frustrated and didn't feel that the meetings were going well, but they couldn't really articulate what they needed to feel more successful.

In the meantime Kim felt the culture shifting and noticed teachers were complaining and seemed to be less engaged. She shared her worries about staff morale with the coaches and asked them for help in identifying both the problem and solutions. The coaches were honest and told her that the PLC leaders needed more clarity and support to effectively lead the team meetings. While there was a structure for leading these meetings, it was deliberately loose to provide teams with some autonomy. The coaches shared that while ultimately this was a good thing, the PLC leaders didn't have enough experience or skills as facilitators. Furthermore, some didn't feel confident in their own use of learning targets with students. Some positive feedback came from Carla, a literacy coach. She shared that the coaching cycle she was currently doing with the language arts department chair was helping not only address student goals, but also was helping the teacher feel more confident in leading her team because she was having success in using learning targets in her classroom. Carla was witnessing firsthand the shifts in the teacher's facilitation skills as she participated in her PLC.

Armed with this information, Kim was able to help the school move forward. She met again with the leadership team and provided information on how to facilitate the development of learning targets. Clear phases were identified so that teams could move more intentionally through the process. She also asked Carla and the teacher to share their story with the team, reminding the team leaders that they had coaches who could provide them with additional support. Finally, during the monthly leadership team meetings, Kim continued to provide professional development (PD) around learning targets and team facilitation. Two months later, not only were team meetings running more effectively, but shifts in classroom instruction and school climate were also visible. The coaches' honesty and support were essential in helping address what could have potentially, if left unchecked, become a culture killer.

WHERE ARE YOU NOW?

Developing and maintaining a healthy culture requires a relentless focus on learning. One barometer of a healthy culture is how well staff work together in pursuit of learning for both students and themselves. The

Figure 4.3   Self-Assessment for School Leaders

Create a Culture of Learning			
	Accomplished	**Developing**	**Novice**
The School Leader	A culture of learning is created, thus creating the conditions for teachers to engage authentically in coaching cycles and other PD. The school leader sets the tone that "we are all learners" and models this behavior throughout all interactions with teachers.	The school lacks a growth mindset among teachers. Thus there are pockets where a culture of learning is beginning, but there is room for improvement. The school leader is working toward developing transparency regarding his or her own learning and development.	The school leader reinforces a more privatized school culture in which teachers hunker down and avoid coaching. There is a lack of trust among teachers.
Success Criteria	I can . . . • Build a positive culture around coaching • Model having a growth mindset • Make my learning transparent • Take risks as a learner • Listen to teachers and ask open-ended questions		

self-assessment found in Figure 4.3 is designed to help leaders identify where they are operating regarding promoting a culture of learning.

Troubleshooting Around a Healthy Culture

The multitude of conversations principals have every day can either build or destroy culture. It is imperative that leaders consider how their words and actions align with the values of the school. Figure 4.4 provides leaders with language to address common issues that arise so that the leader's words promote, not erode, the culture of the school.

THE COACH'S ROLE

Everyone in the school has a role in helping develop a positive culture, but due to the unique role the coach plays in the school, his or her behavior and actions have a significant impact. There are two key things coaches can do to help improve the culture of the school.

Figure 4.4 Language for Promoting a Healthy Culture

If I hear . . .	Then I can say . . .
"Why can't we cancel learning teams this week, we have back to school night."	"This is a busy week. Learning team time is essential to our work so we won't cancel those this week. I have, however, secured parent volunteers to cover duties on Thursday so that you have time in your classroom to catch up."
"Everything is fine. I think (coach) is a great person. I am just too busy right now."	"Tell me a bit more about what why you can't meet with the coach. Once we identify some of the obstacles in your schedule we can figure out how to make this work."
"I feel like I am the only one on my team who comes prepared. It is just easier for me to do this work by myself."	"Have you mentioned this to your team? When was the last time you reviewed norms and/or completed the self-assessment? Let's look at both of these at the next meeting."
"Can't you just tell us exactly what you want us to do and we will do it?"	"I understand you are frustrated by the newness of what you are being asked to do. It is always uncomfortable when you are learning something new. Let's talk about your concerns, and we can go from there. Together we can figure this out."

Speak Truth to Power

Or more simply, be real and honest with your principal. As a coach you have a unique perspective that no one else in the school has. You work arm-in-arm with teachers and are also a part of the leadership team. You get to see both sides of issues from these different perspectives. Sometimes principals, who many have been long removed from the day-to-day demands of teaching in a classroom, don't see or understand the ramifications of decisions. It is up to the coach to help fill in this perspective and share potential pitfalls.

Avoid Playing Both Sides

One of the challenges of being a coach is associated with not having a peer group. You are neither a classroom teacher nor an administrator. This lack of belonging can sometimes lead a coach to try to fit into both groups by engaging in unproductive behaviors. To fit into the teachers' group, you join in on or say nothing when others are complaining about the principal or new initiatives in the school. To align yourself with the principal, you share things about teachers from an evaluative lens.

The most productive thing a coach can do to build and support a positive climate is to avoid engaging in these types of behavior. This doesn't mean that as a coach you won't have concerns about the principal's actions, but rather than participate in bashing the principal in public, share concerns privately. This also doesn't mean that as a coach you won't see things teachers are doing that aren't productive for students, but rather than "tattletale" to the principal your first approach is having a conversation with the teacher.

IN CLOSING

It is no easy task to develop a positive culture in a school. Adding coaches to the mix can easily complicate things, especially if the leader isn't attentive to the impact this position can have on teacher and student learning. Committing to putting teaching and learning front and center, letting coaches do their job in building collective efficacy, developing healthy teams, nurturing a positive relationship with the coach, and recognizing and addressing conflict helps ensure that the coaches impact will be positive.

As leaders in school we would be wise to heed the words of H. Jackson Brown, Jr., "Remember that children, marriages, and flower gardens reflect the kind of care they get." culture of the school is a reflection of how the adults in the school work together. In a healthy culture coaches, teachers, and students thrive. Creating this culture requires a leader who is committed to the work of teaching and learning and understands the coach's role in helping shape an environment where growth is the focal point.

5 Setting Expectations for Authentic Participation in Coaching

"Control leads to compliance; autonomy leads to engagement."

—Daniel Pink

"Should coaching be voluntary or mandatory?" It's a question that we hear from principals on a regular basis. It's also a question that rests on the broader issue of how we set expectations for participation in a coaching effort. Wouldn't it be nice if we could just hire a coach and then watch teachers engage, learn, and grow from this valuable resource? Yet we know that it takes a bit more strategy than that.

How we set expectations for participation varies from school to school. Some principals take an invitational approach, directing coaches to work with teachers who request their assistance. This may create conditions where some teachers will engage and others may never get off the sidelines. Other schools assign coaching to teachers who "need it," possibly those who are new to the profession or are struggling. In a perfect world this strategy would be effective. But in reality, it leads to a myriad of challenges. Let's say we assign coaching to teachers who are new to the profession. Other staff members may assume that coaching isn't for them. Or assigning coaching to teachers who are struggling may make coaching feel evaluative.

The good news is there is an alternative path to setting expectations for participation in coaching. If we frame coaching as being *inclusive*, or for all teachers, then we build on the belief that coaching is about partnering to meet the needs of each and every student. Like so many things, it's about finding the right balance.

WHY IT MATTERS

Coaches Are a Valuable Resource

Engaging teachers in coaching rests squarely on understanding how adult learners create meaning in their day-to-day work. Without this understanding, we run the risk of creating conditions where teachers comply, but may not do so authentically or with any real intention of putting their learning into practice.

Teacher engagement is also a matter of using our resources to their full potential. In a recent panel discussion, an assistant superintendent shared some great advice. She said if we don't use our coaches to their full potential, then they are just highly paid paraprofessionals. We couldn't agree more. We believe that leveraging our coaching team means that school leaders are strategic about setting expectations for participation.

It's Not About Compliance—Adult Learners Need Choice, Ownership, and Autonomy

Creating conditions for authentic engagement in coaching means we have to steer clear of a compliance-driven approach. Compliance takes coaching from a place of inspiration and learning, to one in which teachers are there for all the wrong reasons.

The more that teachers can own their own learning, the more authentic their engagement will be. Much of this comes down to choice. We know it's paramount for students to have choice, but we'd argue that it is equally important for adult learners because choice is about providing teachers with autonomy over their work. This is the beginning to authentic engagement.

In the bestselling book *Drive* (2009), Daniel Pink explains that we can build autonomy by providing choice around task, time, technique, and team. Figure 5.1 provides examples of how choice, ownership, and autonomy can be provided in each of these areas.

Figure 5.1   Providing Choice, Ownership, and Autonomy to Teachers

Where Choice Can Be Provided	How Choice Can Be Provided
Task	Teachers set their own goals for coaching cycles. Goals focus on student learning and begin with "Students will . . ." Putting the goal-setting process under the control of teachers sends the message, "I am here to help you reach your goals for student learning."
Time	Teachers choose when they will participate in a coaching cycle. Using a scheduling structure with a variety of entry points provides teachers with ownership regarding when they would like to engage.
Technique	Teachers choose the instructional practices that they will integrate into their coaching cycle. This provides the opportunity to implement instruction that aligns with both the students' needs, as well as the school and district expectations.
Team	Teachers choose with whom they will collaborate during coaching cycles. This breaks up existing structures such as PLCs, departments, and grade-level teams and provides fresh and purpose-driven groupings.

Accountability Matters

Pink also suggests that accountability is necessary for authentic engagement. He writes, "Encouraging autonomy doesn't mean discouraging accountability. Whatever operating system is in place, people must be accountable for their work" (2009, p. 105). Accountability and expectations go hand-in-hand. We don't have to be heavy handed or top down. Rather, it is our job to compel teachers to engage because it just makes sense to do so.

It won't mean a whole lot if we set expectations and then don't hold teachers accountable for following through. Sure we give lots of autonomy and choice, but when it comes to leading the coaching effort, we need the principal to ensure that the coach is being used to the full potential. This may come in the form of informal check-ins where the principal asks teachers how they've been partnering with the coach. It can be communicated during staff meetings and in other communications. Or the principal may join coaching sessions to send the message that coaching is valued. In the end, what's most important is for the principal to create the conditions for teachers to make the most from this important resource.

Adult Learners Need Respect

Paul Gorski (2008) writes, "In education, we often talk about the deficit perspective—defining students by their weaknesses rather than their strengths" (p. 32). It can be argued that far too often this approach is applied to teachers. This may happen in the subtlest of ways. A principal has noticed that behavior issues are escalating in a certain classroom. So we'd better get that teacher some coaching. Teachers are complaining that their students aren't coming to them prepared by the previous grade level. Again, let's get that teacher some coaching. Or test data are raising concerns regarding student growth and achievement. You guessed it, that teacher needs coaching.

We recognize that these situations occur in many schools and that the inclination to "get that teacher some coaching" is a natural response. But let's acknowledge that building coaching on a foundation of deficits doesn't do a lot to inspire teachers to engage. It will link coaching to teacher evaluation and often leads teachers to become defensive. They may feel as if they are being unfairly judged. They may resist just for the sake of it. Or they may engage in ways that are inauthentic and with no intention of following through on anything that is discussed during the coaching sessions. What a waste of time, effort, and good intentions.

Coaches are common in all economic sectors. Pro athletes have coaches, business leaders have coaches, and even new mothers can get coaching. So why do we make coaching about certain teachers whom we perceive need to be fixed? If we frame coaching as being for all teachers, then we can flip from a deficit to an asset-based perspective by recognizing that every member of the school community is on a continuous path of learning. Starting the school year with the assumption that every teacher will need support in some way is quite different than thinking that some teachers are okay and others need help. Teaching is hard. Expect that there will be challenges. This is where respect begins.

Adult Learners Need Meaning

We often hear questions about how to make sure that teachers continue to implement what they learned from a coach. In other words, will there be traces of the work a few months later? We like to borrow from the work of Wiggins and McTighe (2005) and refer to this as *transfer*. Grant Wiggins famously said, "The point of school is not to get good at school but to effectively parlay what we learned in school in other learning and in life." This notion of transfer also applies to teachers because we want what was learned to become embedded into daily practice *and* to continue to help students grow as learners.

Creating meaning for adult learners is one of the most powerful ways to ensure that transfer occurs. In his famous TedTalk, Simon Sinek (2015) recommends that we begin any new initiative with the "why." If we ask ourselves, "Why is this important? Why does it matter for our students? And why should I care?," then we are able to frame coaching around student learning.

Sinek's concept of "starting with the why" is known as the *Golden Circle* (Figure 5.2). He argues that many organizations make the mistake of starting with the "what" or the "how." For example, this might be revising the curriculum (the what) or working on effective instruction (the how). When we take this approach we break coaching into discrete—and less compelling— nuts and bolts. For example, schools that start with the how often focus on instructional practice in an isolated manner. This leads to a more teacher-centered approach to coaching. Schools that start with the what focus on nitty-gritty expectations, like time commitments and other logistical matters. This leads to a compliance-driven perception among teachers.

We know that the most powerful way to engage teachers in a coaching effort is through the why, because the why is student learning. This makes coaching outcomes-based and also provides a rationale that reaches the soul of teachers. After all, student learning is why we are here in the first place.

Figure 5.2 Simon Sinek's Golden Circle

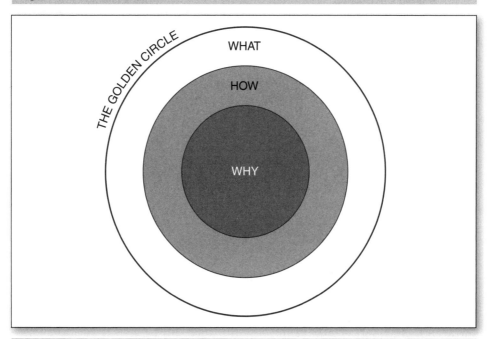

Source: The Golden Circle, recreated by Sally King at SK Graphic Design www.skgraphicdesign.co.uk/. This infographic was adapted by research by Simon Sinek and a TED presentation he delivered called "How Great Leaders Inspire Action." Shared by Gavin Llewellyn under the Creative Commons 2.0 Attribution: https://creativecommons.org/licenses/by/2.0/legalcode via https://www.flickr.com/photos/gavinjllewellyn/6353289537/in/photolist-aFqgCM.

WHAT IT LOOKS LIKE

There are some concrete things that a school leader can do to ensure that coaching impacts teacher and student learning. With these actions, teachers will understand why it matters to step up to the plate and engage as learners.

The first step for the principal is to cultivate a school culture that embraces learning and growth. This then becomes the starting point for teacher engagement. It begins with setting high expectations for student learning, and then holds teachers accountable for reaching those expectations. This creates a high performance culture for students and teachers. Doug Lemov (2010) identifies this as a "no opt out" school culture. He writes, "One consistent finding of academic research is that high expectations are the most reliable driver of high student achievement, even in students who do not have a history of successful achievement" (2010, p. 30).

When we have a culture of high expectations for teachers, then we are focused on doing what's best for each and every student, therefore eliminating the possibility that teachers are doing things as they have been done. We need to establish absolute certainty that the things we are doing are moving students to meet or exceed the standards. It also removes the option for some teachers to sit on the sidelines. A no opt out school culture implies that *everyone* engages in the hard work of doing what's best for students. The following leadership moves will help a principal do just that.

Leadership Move #1: Frame Coaching as Being for All Teachers

Teachers who understand that working with the coach is their professional duty also understand that it is a critical aspect to meeting the students' needs and preparing them academically. It's less than strategic for a school leader to tell the faculty that they are expected to do a coaching cycle and then leave it at that. While there is certainly an expectation set through this message, there isn't a rationale for why it's important. It also isolates teacher development to only coaching cycles. We'd rather present the whole professional learning picture to teachers and provide them with a variety of entry points regarding how they engage.

We advocate for school leaders to set expectations for participation in this way, "As a school we are working on [fill in the blank with your school improvement goal]. There will be many opportunities to learn and grow in this area. We will be learning together during collaboration time, through whole school professional learning and in coaching cycles. I'd like you to engage in a way that meets your needs as a learner and the needs of your students. What matters most is that you stretch yourself and help our school reach the goal that we have set."

Communicating in this way sets up a principal to check in with teachers on a continual basis. Follow up conversations would be framed by questions such as "What have you been trying that aligns with our school goal?" "How are your students growing as a result of your learning?" "What challenges are you still facing?" and "How can I help you get more involved? I'd suggest a coaching cycle." You may have noticed that the teacher isn't being let off the hook regarding engaging as a learner. Rather, the principal guides the teacher to engage on their own terms.

If we ask all teachers to step up to the plate, then we have to meet them with quality coaching. Effective coaching means we understand how to make coaching timely, relevant, and rigorous for every teacher in the school. Coaching sessions are framed by a goal for student learning that has been set by the teacher. Every coaching session is about pushing the students to higher levels of performance. When coaching is relevant and about student performance, it becomes silly to think that some teachers would opt out. This is simply not an option.

Leadership Move #2: Align Coaching With the School Improvement Plan

Let's take a moment to connect the school improvement plan to engagement in coaching. Suppose a school is all over the place when it comes coaching and professional development. One week teachers are learning about a new behavior management system, the next week they are studying a new math program, and so on. When professional learning lacks focus, it is hard for teachers to understand the role of the coach in relationship to that learning. This makes it harder for a coach to get traction with teachers.

Establishing a professional learning focus can typically span a school year. Ideally, the focus is driven by student data as well as teacher input. For example, when making the shift to the Common Core Standards, the teachers at Arrupe Jesuit High School noticed that many students were struggling to write in the content areas. As a result, this became the professional learning focus for all the teachers at the school. The coach supported the teachers to figure out what it looked like for their students. She also helped them implement instructional practices that would be most effective to help students reach the standard. Together they monitored student growth related to the goal. Establishing this focus created a school improvement plan that was informed by teachers, was student-centered, and ensured that coaching was relevant to all teachers.

Leadership Move #3: Expect Coaching Cycles to Be Occurring

This is a simple, but critical, expectation. If coaching cycles aren't occurring, then it will be impossible to create a no opt out school culture. When coaching cycles are missing, opting out is easy because there isn't anything tangible to opt into.

Coaches may be shy about initiating coaching cycles. Or they may be filling their time with other duties such as organizing data, providing resources, or engaging in informal coaching work. Principals can't allow this to happen because when we eliminate our most powerful lever, coaching cycles, then we diminish our impact. We suggest for principals to check in regularly with their coach about cycles and be concerned if they aren't occurring on a regular basis. While every school is different, we think a healthy target is to expect coaches to be spending *most* of their time in coaching cycles. By aiming for *most* of the coach's time, we send a clear message that deep and ongoing work is what we are all about.

Leadership Move #4: Affirm and Celebrate

A no opt out school culture is softened through affirmation and celebration. Affirmation sends the message that the hard work teachers are engaging in has been noticed, affirmed, and appreciated. Consider a learning environment where affirmation is missing. Suppose you took a beginner golf lesson and received no encouragement. Sure your swing may be awful, but the instructor could at least affirm your effort. Or imagine a parent-teacher conference for your good-natured and hard-working son. What if the teacher never mentioned a single nice thing about him? Wouldn't that rub you the wrong way?

It's a sad reality that our schools are deserts when it comes to affirming and celebrating teachers. Teaching is a demanding profession, and if we don't celebrate teachers, then we shouldn't expect a lot in return. Carol Dweck (2006) recommends praising effort rather than ability. She writes, ". . . when students were praised for effort, 90 percent of them wanted the challenging new task that they could learn from" (p. 72). This applies to teachers as well. Affirming effort motivates us to do more, not less.

A simple thing that school leaders can do is to look for things to celebrate each and every day. Sandy is a principal who set a goal of affirming the teachers in her school. This was a new strategy for her because when she was in school for her principal license, she had been taught to avoid singling people out with praise. In her early years as a principal she took this advice and worked hard to stay neutral in her interactions with teachers. But as time passed, Sandy began feeling more and more disconnected from the teachers in her school. This feeling of isolation and lack of connection didn't sit well with her so she tried something different. She tried using affirmation as a strategy to build stronger connections with the teachers.

Her first step was to put a Post-it Note on her computer screen with the simple word "Celebrate" written on it. This served as a reminder to look for celebrations and name them back to teachers as often as possible. Here are some of the other strategies that we recommend:

- Celebrate *all* teachers: Everyone has something worthwhile going on. Keep a chart of who you've connected with in an affirmational way on any given week.
- Spend time in classrooms and during collaboration time: It's hard to know what to celebrate when principals aren't spending time among teachers on a regular basis.
- Be honest: We all know when a compliment isn't authentic. Make your affirmations real by focusing on teachers' effort, their students' growth, or how they are contributing to the school community.

Leadership Move #5: Engage the Unengaged

We are sure that at this point some readers are wondering how to address the issue of teachers who just won't engage, no matter what we do. This is a legitimate challenge that most principals have experienced. It can be frustrating when teachers who would benefit simply won't get involved. You may be tempted to use a parenting strategy and say, "Do it because I said so!" But you know that this is probably not the most conducive way to build a learning community. Instead, let's apply what we know about engaging adult learners and think in different ways about the reasons that might be causing reluctance. Figure 5.3 provides some examples of how to do so.

LESSON FROM THE FIELD

Sarah is an instructional coach in a middle school. Her district is a year and half into a coaching initiative, and they are working hard to ensure that coaching is outcomes-based and student-centered. During a recent PD session with a cohort of coaches focusing on literacy, math, and technology, Sarah raised her hand and asked an innocent enough question. The group had been discussing the importance of principals and coaches meeting regularly to discuss their coaching cycles. With a perplexed look on her face, she said, "I'm confused. Aren't our coaching cycles supposed to be

Figure 5.3 Moves for Encouraging Teachers to Engage in Coaching

Teachers Who Are on a Plan of Improvement	Teachers Who Are Resistant to Change	Teachers Who Lack Self-Efficacy or Confidence
• Send the message that joining in a coaching cycle is valued and expected for everyone in the school • Allow the teacher to decide when the coaching cycle will occur • Continually reinforce your expectations for specific instructional practices to be used by teachers • Affirm and celebrate growth and learning • Engage in a data review with the teacher at the end of the coaching cycle. Discuss how the students grew as well as what the teacher is now implementing	• Reinforce the notion that coaching cycles are designed to move student learning forward rather than to fix teachers • Continually reinforce your expectations for specific instructional practices to be used by teachers • Probe why the teacher may be feeling resistant. Listen and try to address any concerns • Remind the teacher that coaching cycles are a part of what teachers do in the school community • Affirm and celebrate growth and learning	• Encourage the teacher to buddy up with someone they feel comfortable with during the coaching cycle • Help the teacher build content knowledge through PD, Personal Learning Networks (PLNs), and conferences • Remind the teacher that coaching cycles are a part of what teachers do in the school community • Affirm and celebrate growth and learning

kept confidential?" She went on to explain that confidentiality had been discussed at length in the early stages of their coaching initiative. It was an ironclad rule. One that everyone agreed was essential if coaches had any chance of building trust with teachers. The hope was that by taking this approach they would get people to participate because coaching wouldn't feel evaluative. They didn't want teachers to feel threatened by coaching, so they keep it quiet.

Diane had just begun working with Sarah's cohort, and she didn't want to dismiss decisions that had been made before she became involved. She probed the coaching team to find out how their recent experiences lined up with the notion that coaching should be confidential. Matthew weighed in, "The idea of confidentiality seems to fit more with a teacher-centered approach to coaching. It also feels kind of negative." Diane nodded and suggested that they rethink this notion of confidentiality, especially since they were being so intentional about framing coaching as being student-centered.

As they continued their discussion, another coach wondered if Diane would be willing to bring this up with their team of principals. Otherwise, they may not be on the same page. She agreed and mentioned that she would be meeting with Sarah's principal the following morning. She would get his input and then bring the conversation to the rest of the principals in the afternoon.

The next morning, Rob, Sarah, and Diane sat down together for their second school-based consultancy of the year. These sessions were geared toward helping Rob develop systems and structures for the coaching effort. While Rob was an experienced principal and had been at the school for 10 years, this was his first time with a full-time coach.

It was one of those grey and chilly mornings in early December. The focus for the meeting was how to relaunch coaching after the winter break. Diane began the conversation by sharing, "Sarah asked a great question yesterday. She wondered what my thoughts were about keeping coaching cycles confidential. What do you think?" Sarah nodded and turned to hear Rob's response. He smiled and said, "That's a good question. I can see both sides of it. We wouldn't want teachers to feel like they are being judged or evaluated, I get that. My issue is that I feel like Sarah and I are limited in how well we can work together if coaching is confidential. I'd like to be an active participant, but I also don't want to jeopardize her relationships with the teachers."

Diane added that keeping coaching confidential might create challenges when it comes to setting expectations for participation. Since coaching isn't about "fixing" teachers, we'd hate to give the impression that there's something to hide. She said, "Since we are thinking about how we will relaunch coaching in January, what if we addressed the issue of confidentiality then? What if we set the tone that coaching is for everyone and is therefore not something we have to keep confidential?" Rob nodded and replied, "I'd still want the teachers to understand that they can trust the process." "Absolutely," said Diane, "that's the bedrock of everything we do."

As they continued their meeting, they sketched out some key messages that Rob would share with the teachers when they got back from break. These key messages would lead toward authentic participation in the next round of coaching cycles:

- Coaching is for everyone. If you haven't had a chance to participate, please consider doing so now.
- Your coaching goal is up to you. Please choose something that feels important to you and your students.
- Sarah will be launching a new round of coaching cycles in a week. Please follow up with her to get on her schedule.

- You will have another chance to join a coaching cycle in March. Again, if you haven't participated, please do so.
- As the principal, I'd like to know what you are working on with Sarah. She will share the great things you are doing and how your students are growing. Please let her know if this makes you uncomfortable.
- Remember we are a learning community. We all have room to learn and grow.

By making this adjustment, Rob took a big step toward framing coaching as being open, transparent, and driven by teachers. Suddenly, the question of confidentiality seemed to be far less important because their goal would be to encourage all teachers to see the value in, and engage in, the coaching effort.

Sometimes this isn't as straightforward as it was for Rob. Sometimes teachers camp out on the sidelines with no intention of engaging. This is particularly concerning in situations when the teacher is struggling to provide high quality instruction, or when the students are performing below the desired level. When these situations occur (which they will), it is helpful to think of them as an off ramp toward more direct supervision. If a coach cannot make inroads, then it's time for the leader to step in.

WHERE ARE YOU NOW?

There are some concrete things that principals can do to set expectations for participation in coaching. We suggest using the following rubric to self-assess and set goals around these important leadership moves (Figure 5.4).

Troubleshooting Around Teacher Participation in Coaching

It can take some time to develop a school culture where teachers find value and participate authentically in coaching. In the meantime, principals face an unpredictable landscape where they will find it necessary to frame and reframe their expectations for teacher engagement. Figure 5.5 provides language to support principals through these conversations.

THE COACH'S ROLE

With clear expectations in place, the coach is set up to design systems and structures for coaching cycles. We suggest a predictable (yet flexible) system for scheduling 4 to 6 weeklong coaching cycles. In this way, a coach

Figure 5.4 Self-Assessment for School Leaders

Set Expectations for Authentic Participation in Coaching			
	Accomplished	**Developing**	**Novice**
The School Leader	The principal frames coaching as being for all teachers because all teachers have students with needs. The school leader encourages teachers to engage in coaching cycles and celebrates growth that occurs as a result of cycles.	The principal frames coaching cycles as either "mandated" or "invitational." As a result, some teachers participate authentically, some choose to opt out, and others may participate in a compliance-driven fashion.	The principal leaves it up to the coach to set expectations for participation in coaching cycles. Teachers view coaching as something that doesn't really include or affect them. Certain teachers participate and others steer clear.
Success Criteria	I can . . . • Speak with the full faculty about the importance of coaching and how it will impact student learning. • Create choice, ownership, and autonomy for how teachers engage in coaching cycles. • Celebrate teachers who are engaging and learning from coaching cycles. • Work with the coach to develop systems and resources for engaging teachers in coaching cycles.		

Figure 5.5 Language for Setting Expectations for Participation in Coaching

If I hear . . .	Then I can say . . .
"Why would I need a coach? I've been teaching here since the school opened."	"I appreciate your commitment to our school. Now that we are taking a student-centered approach to coaching, we view it as being a great resource for all teachers. For example, you might work with your coach when you are about to start a unit that has challenged your students in the past. Or you might want to work with your coach on the new science standards. We are all learning how to tap into this important resource and we all have students with diverse needs."
"Does this mean that the coach is going to report what I'm doing in my classroom?"	"My hope is that coaching isn't something that lives in the shadows. I believe that since coaching is student-centered, you'll have a lot of student growth to celebrate. These are important conversations to have."
"Isn't the coach for the new teachers?"	"Coaching is for everyone in our school. New, veteran, all subjects. We all have students with needs, and your coaches are in a great position to help you get there."

can make the message that "coaching is for all teachers" a reality. Here's what we suggest:

Divide the School Year Into Rounds for Coaching Cycles

Each round is a window of time when coaching cycles are offered to teachers. Typically, coaches refer to their curriculum and assessment calendar to determine when their rounds will begin and end. In this way, coaching cycles are aligned to the units that we teach. Many coaches wait to begin their first round until teachers have settled into the school year. Others are sure to include some space between rounds so that they can reflect, recruit a new group of teachers, and manage other necessary duties.

Figure 5.6 provides an example of this structure. In this case, the coach used the month of September to build relationships, help with assessments, and get on the same page with the principal. As soon as October arrived, coaching cycles were in full swing.

Figure 5.6   Example of Coaching Cycle Rounds

Round 1: October to early November

Round 2: Mid-November to early December

Round 3: January to mid-February

Round 4: March to mid-April

Determine How Many Coaching Cycles You Can Handle in Each Round

The amount of cycles will vary based on the coach's duties. The upper limit for many coaches is four cycles during a round. Going past this target can become too much and lead to a coach feeling overwhelmed. It's also important to remember that coaching cycles are suggested to occur with between one and three teachers. If a coach is in two schools, then two coaching cycles in each school would be a good goal. Again, this means that the coach would be working with between two and six teachers in each school.

Invite Teachers to Participate

A few weeks before a new round begins, an invitation goes out to teachers to encourage them to participate. If a coach notices that certain teachers aren't joining in, then a gentle nudge of encouragement may be delivered by the principal. As coaching cycles get up and running, the coach may collect testimonials to encourage others to engage in the future. This may be just what a hesitant teacher needs to trust the process and become involved.

Teachers who get used to this system come to understand that there will be many opportunities to engage in coaching cycles and that it's up to them to decide when it makes the most sense. It might be that a teacher wants to work with a coach later in the year when she teaches a unit that has been challenging in the past. Or perhaps a teacher may decide to do a coaching cycle right at the beginning of the year because he knows it's a great way to start strong.

Create a Schedule for Coaching Cycles

With a list of participating teachers in hand, the coach creates a schedule for the upcoming round of coaching cycles. While there are some things that remain consistent throughout the year (such as the principal and coach meeting, PLCs, etc.), the schedule for coaching cycles changes with each round. This provides the opportunity for the coach to make adjustments as the school year progresses. Perhaps the coach did a few too many cycles and wants to scale back. Or maybe the coach can ramp things up a bit and add more. Recreating the schedule for each round allows the coach to continually refine his or her schedule to best meet the needs of teachers.

Engage in Coaching Cycles

With this information in place, the coach is set up for a successful round of coaching cycles. As the cycles come to a close, we recommend an exit interview to reflect on how the teacher and students grew throughout the process. Then it's time to relaunch coaching cycles with a whole new group of teachers. A fresh start!

IN CLOSING

For too long, coaching has been viewed as something to avoid. When this is the case, it sure is hard to build a collaborative culture that embraces, and gets the most out of, a coaching effort. A more profound impact would be widespread participation by teachers that is authentic and meaningful. Participating just for the sake of it isn't enough, not if we hope to make a positive impact on student and teacher learning.

While we believe that mandating coaching leads to a compliance-driven model where teachers seem to engage but may not transfer learning to their ongoing practice, we also know that if coaching is too invitational, then only pockets of teachers may be involved. Again, this fails to make use of this precious resource.

Let's think about how we might truly engage the adult learners in our school. If we begin here, then we can help teachers participate authentically while also fostering a collaborative school culture. In this way, coaching will become the way we do business, because it will honor teachers' choice, autonomy, and their sense of self. Now we are onto something: engagement that reaches the soul of a teacher. Engagement that will truly make a difference in teaching and learning.

6 Driving Toward High Quality Instruction

"Leadership and learning are indispensable to each other."

—John F. Kennedy

There is a popular show on TLC called *Cake Boss*. Watching the team of bakers put their elaborate masterpieces together evokes what needs to happen in schools that have student-centered coaches. As the name implies there was a "boss" or lead baker who was intimately involved in designing and making the cakes. Central to making sure the plan was carried out were bakers who had specialized skills such as making delicate frosting flowers. Driving a school toward high quality instruction requires a differentiated skill set much like that of the cake boss and his bakers. Principals need to be intimately involved in understanding curriculum and pedagogy, but their expertise alone isn't enough. Their hands need to be in the mix, kneading and monitoring the instruction in the school. Then the coaches put the finer edges on instruction by working alongside teachers to ensure that the batter is just right.

Combining the skill sets of the principal and coach ensures that the goals of the school will be met. The challenge is in making sure that the principal and coach are adept at working together to develop and support high quality instruction throughout the school.

WHY IT MATTERS

Clarity Promotes Learning

The first step in baking is to determine the type of cake you are going to create, this dictates the ingredients and tools that are needed. The same holds true for improving instruction. The first step is to define what you want for students in the school. Knowing this guides us toward the instructional model. It is why mission and vision work is more than a "nice to have" but "have to have" because it helps determine the focus for curriculum, instructional strategies, and assessments. These are the cornerstones of an instructional model, but just like the flavor of a cake is determined by how the ingredients interact, instructional models must be coherent. This means there needs to be coordination within and between grade levels for these three variables to make schools work (Robinson, 2011). Coherence of this nature promotes achievement for students because it helps kids connect with prior learning and experiences (Bansford, Brown, & Cocking, 2000). A coherent instructional model means that teachers reinforce the same ideas, use similar vocabulary for communicating these ideas, and link previous learning. Students achieve at higher rates because learning is integrated and connected rather than fragmented or disjointed.

When it comes to teacher learning, the same logic holds true. If teachers are going to improve their practice, then they need professional learning experiences that are integrated and send a consistent message about effective teaching. A coherent instructional model provides clarity for not only students, but also teachers because it narrows their learning agenda. Rather than chase the flavor of the month or year, a coherent instructional model serves as the catalyst for the adult learning in the school. With a coherent instructional model in place the principal and coach have a focused way forward, ensuring that they are both working toward baking the same cake. Without this schools run the risk of initiative overload causing confusion and fatigue; overwhelming even the most engaged teachers. The intimate nature of coaching cycles, coupled with the fact that the majority of coaches work across grade levels, provides a unique vantage point that the principal needs to help achieve coherence across the school.

You Are Not a Superhero

The good news is that we know more than ever about the principal behaviors that result in positive outcomes for students (Robinson, 2011). And not surprisingly these behaviors fall into the category of instructional leadership, or more simply put, leading learning. The bad news is that in many school systems, this research has led to a myopic focus on day-to-day instruction. Principals feel enormous pressure to be the superhero of teaching and learning, swooping in to micromanage instruction by using data as their special superpower. While tending to instruction is important, after all learning is the business of schools, it isn't humanly possible for one person to shoulder this responsibility. When this happens, leaders tend to narrow their focus on instruction and student achievement, creating blind spots to other critical aspects of leading learning such as promoting focused collaboration or building capacity (Fullan, 2014).

Improving instruction throughout the school requires a one, two punch. Principals provide one punch by developing the professional capital of teachers and supporting and motivating them to work together productively. Coaches provide the second punch by working with teachers so that the students' needs are met through effective classroom instruction. This doesn't mean that principals shouldn't understand best practices in curriculum, instruction, and assessment. They most certainly need to be adept in these areas if they are going to provide clarity and focus, but like in *Cake Boss*, they leave some of the nuances to the coach. One of the strongest principal and coach teams we've worked with had a principal with a strong instructional background, she was well read, understood the curriculum, and had intimate knowledge of what effective practices should look and sound like. The coach was also highly trained and was well versed in understanding the intricacies in helping students who were struggling. The one-two punch of this coach principal team resulted in rich learning for teachers and students.

"People" Not "Programs"

Even with all the latest advancements in medical technology you would never hear people say, "Thank goodness for those medical instruments. They saved my life." That's absurd. When a patient improves, it is attributed to the doctor because it's the person, not the tool, who makes the difference. And yet in a frenzied sense of urgency to improve test scores, principals and districts find themselves looking for the latest and greatest fix that will cure all the schools' ills. This may come in the form of new curriculum or technology, with the hope that purchasing the programs will magically improve student achievement.

Just as medical instruments don't save lives, programs don't teach students how to read or understand complex problems. Teachers do. But teachers, like doctors, need to be highly skilled, and this requires more than putting a set of directions in their hands. It requires being adept at knowing what students need, when they need it, and then using the right tools to make that happen. This complexity demands a multidimensional, all hands on deck approach to teacher learning.

Fullan (2014) describes this complexity when talking about the principal's role in leading instruction,

> [T]hey should get at it by working with teachers individually and collectively to develop *their* professional capital. . . . The principal is in there by helping the group get good. The question is what combination of factors will maximize that press for most teachers' learning and therefore for most students' learning? (p. 73)

The answer to these questions is not determined by figuring out which is the best program or technology to purchase. Rather, it lies in the partnership between the coach and principal working in tandem to develop both human and social capital.

WHAT IT LOOKS LIKE

Driving toward high quality instruction requires a partnership between the principal and the coach. The success of this partnership hinges on the principal understanding his or her role in leading learning. Setting and monitoring expectations means a leader has a firm grip on effective practices in curriculum and instruction. The leadership moves described here will set the principal on the path to making this happen.

Leadership Move #1: Seek Clarity, Not Compliance

Identifying an instructional model and then not using it to support teacher and student learning is like gardeners who never water, weed, or fertilize their garden. Having an instructional model is critical as we stated earlier in this chapter, but driving toward consistency and precision in instruction requires more than just planting the seed. Making the instructional model come to life requires attention and support and this begins with promoting clarity not compliance.

Clarity requires not only having a deep understanding of what the practice looks and sounds like, but also knowing when it makes the most sense to use the practice. Getting to this level of understanding requires deep learning that can only be achieved when teachers have had time to wrestle with the concepts inside the classroom (with the help of a coach) and outside the classroom (with the help of the learning team).

One of the biggest impediments to this process is the use of checklists to monitor the instructional program. Checklists promote compliance in that they are focused on whether or not the practice is present, they can't discern whether or not the practice will make a difference, nor do they lend themselves to effective feedback. When Ann's boys were taking driver's education they had a 16-point checklist they needed to complete before starting the car. While this helped them get the car started properly, it was no guarantee that they would be able to navigate the roads successfully.

Rather than checklists, we promote the use of look fors to go after clarity. Look fors are clear statements that describe an observable teaching or learning behavior, strategy, outcome, product, or procedure (Mooney & Mausbach, 2008). Look fors bridge the gap between learning and implementation because they help teachers understand the target. Figure 6.1 outlines the differences between a checklist and look fors.

Figure 6.1 Difference Between Checklists and Look Fors

	Checklist	Look Fors
Purpose	To determine whether or not a step or concept is in place	Clearly state in observable terms what the teaching practice, process, behavior, and strategy look like and sound like when implemented so that teachers develop a shared understanding
Development	Typically focus on a generic set of instructional practices	Based on the school improvement and professional development plan and are developed collaboratively after a staff has engaged in learning
Feedback Focus	Focused on quantifiable results, such as whether or not the item was observed or present	Validate practice through describing what was observed that matched look fors and why that matters, also promotes reflection
Example of Feedback From the Principal	"When I observed in your class today, seven out of ten students were completing the task assigned."	"During your focus lesson I observed how you used a think aloud to share examples and counterexamples. This is so useful for students especially when they are just learning a new math concept. This really helps them create mental pictures in their minds. How do you think your think aloud will change as you move to more abstract concepts?"
Example of Feedback From the Coach	Not Applicable: Coaches should not be engaged in using checklists to observe teachers because it is an evaluative process.	"Last time we met we were discussing how to help our students self-assess their progress on learning targets. As we examine student work let's keep in mind the professional learning we had last week on this same topic since this is one of our school's looks fors."

When look fors are used in conjunction with walk-throughs, they provide context and lead to more effective feedback. Look fors help coaches because they provide a common starting point for everyone in the school. For example, if using formative assessment data to respond to student needs is the focus for the school, then providing feedback with a checklist on engagement isn't going to result in increased use of formative assessments. It might increase the level of engagement, but it won't help teachers get better at responding to students. To do that, teachers need to know upfront what the practice looks and sounds like. Then they need feedback that validates and helps them reflect on their use of this practice. Figure 6.2 provides an example of look fors that have been developed around different school improvement initiatives.

Figure 6.2 Examples of Look Fors

Focus of the School Improvement Plan	Examples of Look Fors
Higher Order Thinking	• Teacher consistently asks higher level questions and expects students to explain their thinking. • Student thinking is evident in work (graphic organizers, concept maps, etc.). • Displays of student work include purpose and rationale for assignments and demonstrate student thinking. • Teacher models using a think aloud and guides student learning through the process (concepts and strategies). • Engagement in authentic learning tasks is evident. • Students can articulate the purpose (big idea or major concept) of the lesson.

Small Group Instruction	• Teacher uses prompts, cues, and questions when students are working in small groups.
	• Students show evidence of a focused lesson through:
	   ○ Partner discussion, i.e., students are talking about what was learned during the lesson.
	   ○ Students are using books or materials that were supplied for guided practice so the teacher can check for understanding.
	   ○ Students are using the skill or strategy from the focus lesson.
	   ○ Peers are supporting each other through questioning.

Focus Lesson	• Teacher uses intentional or precise language and provides a singular, clear curricular objective that includes purpose and application. • Teacher consistently contains "I" statements (not "you" statements). • Teacher focuses on his or her own expert thinking process (not directions) to apprentice students to teacher thinking. • Teacher establishes relevance of the purpose beyond the classroom or for learning's sake. • Lesson is 10 minutes to 15 minutes in length and appropriate for the age group.

Leadership Move #2: Collaboratively Develop Look Fors

The use of collaboratively developed look fors unifies a school by helping create shared meaning and a common focus. On the surface the development of look fors is a conceptually simple, straightforward practice. However, there are complexities to the process, and if these are ignored, they may render the look fors irrelevant. Mausbach and Morrison (2016) outline four keys to developing look fors.

1. *Look fors are collaboratively developed by all staff.* The purpose of having a set of look fors is to help staff understand what the strategies will look like when they are in place. In a heightened sense of urgency to get the look fors developed, a leader may be tempted to create the list and hand it out. Or even worse, use some developed by another school. Both practices are harmful because they remove the staff's opportunity to learn. It also promotes the mentality that the coach is the expert. It is both the process and the product that matter. Developing look fors as a faculty helps the staff develop shared meaning, clarify misconceptions, and deepen ownership.

2. *Look fors are directly connected to the school improvement plan.* Look fors promote clarity by helping operationalize the school improvement plan. Thus, look fors must describe the strategies in the plan. Effective school improvement plans provide focus for a school, and aligned look fors are essential for intense focus.

3. *Look fors can't be developed in the absence of knowledge, but understand it is a developmental process.* One of the biggest benefits of developing look fors is that the process deepens teachers' understanding of the initiative that is being implemented. This happens by engaging staff in learning around the initiative before developing the list. Without providing time for learning, the look fors may not be detailed or useful enough to provide feedback. The saying "You don't know what you don't know" is apropos here. Deep meaning will occur as they implement, and learning is the work (Fullan, 2009). Look fors are a vehicle for learning, and understanding will develop as teachers work with coaches and the principal to develop look fors.

4. *Look fors are observable.* Look fors can be seen or heard. They provide evidence of strategy implementation. They also help a leader

focus observations so meaningful feedback can be provided. Consider the difference between the following look fors:

Look for A: Evidence of rigor and relevance

Look for B: Students know the purpose for learning and can articulate thinking strategies. (p. 80)

Look for A leaves too much to interpretation, while Look for B provides a more specific expectation. Armed with this specificity, principals and coaches can work together to support teachers as they work toward meeting these expectations. The key is to make sure that look fors are observable.

Leadership Move #3: Don't Ignore the What

When it comes to leading for action, effective principals understand that it is critical to start with the why (Sinek, 2009); however, the what and how are also an integral part of the equation. As outlined in Chapter 5, this is essential because it creates meaning. The key is to pay attention to both the how and what in relation to the why. In schools it is easy to emphasize developing strong instructional skills, or the how. This makes sense because teaching is complex and it takes a long time to get good at it. However, good instruction can't compensate for a weak curriculum, or the what. Schmoker (2011) says it best, "Even the best pedagogy can't overcome the negative effects of incoherent curriculum, just as the best exercise regimen can't overcome the damage done by eating fast food" (p. 70).

Implementing a common curriculum with clear, intelligible standards isn't a one and done activity. Having standards, while a starting point, isn't enough. Having curriculum maps or guides developed by the district office aren't enough either. These are essential, but what is really required, if the curriculum is going to be effective, is for teachers to make sense of it and to use it in ways that helps their students learn. This happens through use and reflection, the reflection that is inherent in effective PLCs and coaching cycles. Figure 6.3 provides guiding questions that principals and coaches can use as they support teachers in making sure there is a coherent curriculum.

Leadership Move #4: Lead From a Learner Stance

As we stated earlier in the chapter, leaders can't be the superheroes of instruction. One way to avoid donning the cape is to be a student of teaching and learning. Learning with staff, and from the coach, are essential

Figure 6.3 Guiding Questions That Focus on Curriculum

Principal

During Walk-Throughs

- Is student learning aligned with the standards?
- Is instruction aligned with the curriculum maps?
- Do students understand the learning target?
- Do learning targets match learning activities?

During Collaboration

- Is there clarity on what students should know and do during this unit?
- How do we know students are learning the curriculum?
- What will we do to help students who haven't learned?

Coach

During Collaboration

- How does the student work support students understanding of the standards?
- Do we have clear learning targets that align to the standard(s)?
- How will we address misconceptions on learning targets?

During Coaching Cycles

- What are the learning targets for our students?
- Which standards do they address?

practices. This means attending professional development meetings at the district level alongside staff as well as those hosted at the school site. We once worked with a principal who had been a high school language arts teacher. After his first year as a principal, he understood that to be effective, he had to learn more about effective practices in other content areas, specifically math. He asked the coach who had a math background for suggestions on what books he should read so he could spend his summer digging in. In the fall, he carved out extra time with the coach so they could discuss his new learning and apply it to what he was seeing in his walk-throughs. Not only does the leader's competence deepen through these practices, it also models for the staff that it is okay to ask for support from the coach.

Leadership Move #5: Help Coaches Stay on Track

One of the greatest things about working with coaches is their unbridled enthusiasm for all things teaching and learning. Many coaches are drawn to this position because of their love and dedication to effective teaching.

This enthusiasm is extremely beneficial, but if left unchecked it can lead a school down an unwanted path. Most coaches tend toward being voracious consumers of professional reading, Twitter, and other online sources. They can get caught up in trying to implement great ideas that may not be practical in the context of their own school at that particular moment in time.

The way to help coaches stay on track is by implementing practices suggested throughout this book (i.e., having a clear plan, meeting with them weekly) and also by not being afraid to say no. Steve is a principal who works with a coach who loves technology and has a background in gifted education. He has a rich online presence via blogs and Twitter where he engages with others about new and innovative practices. He offers a great perspective to the team, but the principal finds herself saying no to him frequently because many times the school isn't ready for what he wants to initiate, nor does it align with the school improvement plan. The coach and principal meet on a weekly basis so they have a strong relationship, which makes these conversations easier, but it still requires the principal to be a bit of gatekeeper, saying no or not yet, when necessary.

LESSON FROM THE FIELD

Amy had been a principal for a couple of years when she was transferred to a new school. She knew she was inheriting a school that had committed teachers who were not used to major changes. In addition to having a new principal for the first time in over a decade, the district was adopting a basal series in reading for the first time in over 20 years. Amy knew that any initiatives in the school improvement plan needed to be clear and focused for her staff to be on board. The leadership team, which consisted of the principal, coaches, and teachers representing each grade level, decided to focus on using learning intentions. Learning intentions are signposts or objectives shared with the students about what they should be learning as a result of doing. This focus was chosen because it would help improve instructional practices, which test results indicated were needed, and also because Amy didn't want the new basal reading series to drive instruction.

Amy and the two coaches met weekly to plan and provide weekly professional development around learning intentions. Through the coaches' work in coaching cycles and Amy's daily walk-throughs, they came to the same conclusion. Teachers were having difficulty understanding the difference between "I can" statements and learning intentions. Learning intentions were becoming activities rather than the *what* and *why* of learning. A few teachers hoped to be told exactly what they needed to do. They asked how many times they should refer to the learning intention in a lesson, if they needed to post it, and if so, how? They wanted to do things just right and requested some clear-cut answers.

Amy and the coaches brainstormed why the teachers were feeling so unsure and what they could do about it. They concluded that part of the issue was motivated by fear of doing something wrong. They knew that they had to provide support to help the teachers work through this, and they also wanted to continue to encourage teachers to take risks. At the next PD meeting, Amy and the coaches went back to the research and provided teachers with examples and nonexamples of learning intentions. But before they did so, they had a discussion about why they are important. Discussing the why helped teachers see that there were no clear-cut "numbers" they needed to hit in regards to use. Finally, the school developed a set of look fors around learning intentions, which turned into a rubric to help guide them as they worked through the process.

This work helped the teachers get unstuck, with the exception of one teacher who had lost her confidence and was feeling a bit "beat up." She wanted no part of coaching, and asked Amy to tell her what to do so she could just do it. Amy spent a lot of time with this teacher, observing her and validating the practices that she was using. Through their conversational feedback, the teacher began to open up and feel less threatened. Over time she began to come to Amy with questions. Rather than answer them directly, Amy suggested that these were the types of issues the coach could help her address. Finally, the teacher asked for a coaching cycle and was thrilled when her students went from 15% to 70% proficiency on the district assessment. In Amy's second year at the school, the teacher and her team requested a coaching cycle at the beginning of the year because they knew it would get their year off to a great start. Amy's leadership led to literacy scores that were the highest they had been in 3 years, and the teachers were more comfortable taking risks to make sure that their students were learning. Having a clear plan, developing look fors around instructional practice, working in partnership with coaches, and providing feedback to teachers paid off for Amy and her team.

WHERE ARE YOU NOW?

Working toward high quality instruction requires a strong partnership between the principal and the coach. They need a strong complementary skill set to ensure a coherent instructional program. Figure 6.4 is a tool that leaders can use to assess their progress regarding leading teaching and learning in partnership with the coach.

Figure 6.4 Self-Assessment for School Leaders

Understands Pedagogy and Curriculum Content			
	Accomplished	**Developing**	**Novice**
The School Leader	Expectations for instructional practice are clearly set and defined. Practices are aligned with the school improvement plan. The coach's role is to provide support so that teachers can meet this expectation.	Expectations for the instructional practice are clearly set and defined. Practices are aligned with the school improvement plan. The coach's role is to provide support so that teachers can meet this expectation.	The school leader takes a hands-off approach to leading instruction, allows the teachers to make decisions, and lays little groundwork regarding what is expected.
	The school leader has a well-developed pedagogical understanding and is able to recognize and provide feedback to teachers in direct relationship to the expected teaching practices.	The school leader has a developing sense of pedagogy and may understand some areas of instruction better than others. The school leader is able to provide specific feedback in some areas but not all.	The school leader lacks pedagogical understanding and is therefore unable to provide teachers with specific expectations and feedback regarding instruction.
	The school leader understands the curriculum and what it means for students.	The school leader understands some, but not all, of the curriculum that is used in the school.	The school leader does not understand the curriculum that is used in the school.
Success Criteria	I can . . . • Recognize effective instructional practice across subjects and content areas. • Spend time in classrooms to look for the use of effective instructional practice. • Work in partnership with the coach in service to teaching and learning. • Set the expectation that teachers are implementing effective instructional practice as well as the curriculum. • Learn and grow my understanding of effective instructional practice. • Learn and grow my understanding of the content and curriculum.		

Troubleshooting Around Driving Toward High Quality Instruction

Keeping teaching and learning at the center of the work requires a high degree of vigilance in promoting best practice. Striving toward instructional improvements will be met with many questions as teachers work toward understanding the why, what, and how. How the principal addresses these questions will help determine the success of improvement

Figure 6.5   Language for Driving Toward High Quality Instruction

If I hear . . .	Then I can say . . .
"Why do we need to follow a curriculum map? The district purchased these expensive materials, and we should follow them as instructed."	"There are a couple of reasons we need to use the curriculum map. First, we want to ensure that all students have the opportunity to learn all the standards. The maps are both vertically and horizontally aligned. Second, the district materials are resources and not a curriculum. They are designed to provide support for instruction, but not to drive it."
"Why can't the coach just come in and teach my class for a couple of days? After observing him I should be able to use the practice just fine."	"Our coaching model is centered on student learning. If you are not seeing a positive impact with your students when you use this practice, I am sure the coach would love to sit down with you and work through a coaching cycle. I am also available to come watch you teach and provide feedback."
"I was working with the coach, and she told me not to worry too much about implementing this practice because she just attended a workshop and we are going to start working on something else."	"I haven't had a chance to talk to the coach yet, and I am looking forward to hearing about what she learned. Remember our mantra here though; the work isn't finished until 100% of students benefit from the innovation. We aren't there yet so we can't move on to something new just yet. However, I am sure the coach's new learning will be useful to us in the future."

efforts. Figure 6.5 provides some guidance on how to keep the dialogue focused and productive.

THE COACH'S ROLE

The sole purpose of having coaches is to work with teachers to help improve outcomes for students. But like the principalship, this isn't a job coaches can do on their own. Making this happen requires a strong principal and coach relationship where both are working together to help advance the teaching and learning in the school. There are several key things coaches can do to ensure that their actions support quality instruction across the school.

See, Understand, and Help Advance the Big Picture

Moving out of the classroom and into a coaching position changes perspectives by sheer virtue of a new vantage point. As a classroom teacher, the focus is on what is occurring in the confines of the classroom. As a coach, this lens broadens. Since coaches work across grade levels and content areas, they see the scope of teaching and learning in a way that is impossible to do from just one classroom. "It's hard to see the forest for the trees" applies here. Teachers see the trees; coaches need to see the whole forest so they can understand their role in helping make both the trees and the forest strong and healthy. They do this by helping define and clarify the instructional model and staying true to it when implementing practices via coaching cycles and small group collaboration.

Be a Champion for Curriculum Coherence

Coaches are really the eyes and ears of curriculum coherence. The deep dives they do when working alongside teachers allows them to more easily see when content isn't sequenced correctly, standards are only partially covered, or assessments don't measure what is intended. Thus, one of the biggest impacts they can have is helping uncover, document, and correct areas where the curriculum isn't on track. Coaches do this in two important ways. First, discussing curriculum disconnects should be an ongoing item on the principal and coach agenda. This helps take care of easily solvable issues that can be addressed at the building level, such as helping teachers make sure they understand all parts of a standard. The second way that coaches help is by serving as active members on district curriculum teams. When curriculum revisions are being discussed coaches should be in the room sharing what they have learned since they have a front row seat in seeing how the curriculum impacts learning in the classroom.

Seek Process Advice From Principal

Just as principals should seek out coaches for help in deepening their understanding of curriculum and instructional practices, coaches should seek out principals for advice on working with adults and facilitating groups. Principals' experience and training in leading adults helps coaches leverage their instructional skills in a way that is meaningful to teachers. Working with adults is different than working with children and can be challenging, especially if these dynamics get ignored. Seeking advice and input from the principal on using protocols, keeping conversations focused on goals, and valuing input from everyone in the group will help the coach as he or she hones these important skills.

IN CLOSING

When thinking about what it takes to be a good teacher the Tom Hanks quote from *A League of Their Own* comes to mind, "It's supposed to be hard. If it were easy everyone would be doing it." Teaching is hard work. It is both an art and a science that requires ongoing learning and support. Providing this learning and support is exactly why being a principal is such hard work. Helping teachers hone their craft isn't something leaders can do on their own, just as becoming a better teacher rarely happens in isolation.

When principals and coaches work together toward a shared vision of effective teaching and learning the results are as prized as the masterpieces of the cake boss and his bakers. Nothing is sweeter than seeing students thrive, and this is what happens when the differentiated skill sets of principals and coaches mix. Using the key ingredients of focus and collaboration, principals and coaches are able to inspire teachers and students to reach new heights.

7 Separating Coaching From Supervision

"A garden requires patient labor and attention. Plants do not grow merely to satisfy ambitions or to fulfill good intentions. They thrive because someone expended effort on them."

—Liberty Hyde Bailey

The complexity of leading a school filled with adults and students with diverse needs is analogous to tending to a variety of plants in a garden. The job of the leader, like that of the gardener, is to develop supports and structures that help everyone in the system grow and develop. Gardens and schools prosper when there is a balance between knowing when to water and fertilize, and knowing when to weed. Leaders have to be adept at both. It is easy to get into trouble when the lines between support and evaluation get blurred, something that may be especially tempting when a school has an instructional coach on staff.

Separating coaching from supervision is essential for a coaching effort to take root and thrive. Given the demands of the principalship, and the size and diversity of many teaching staffs, it isn't all that surprising to find principals leaning on coaches to support the supervision process. Using coaches in this capacity undermines the important work of developing a staff and has negative consequences on the culture of the school. This chapter articulates strategies for leading by using effective supervision practices, while supporting student-centered coaching so that everyone gets what they need to grow.

WHY IT MATTERS

Adult Learning Requires Vulnerability

Brené Brown (2012) writes, "The big challenge for leaders is getting our heads and hearts around the fact that we need to cultivate the courage to be uncomfortable and to teach the people around us how to accept discomfort as part of growth" (p. 199). Vulnerability for teachers is being open to new ideas, admitting not knowing how to help a struggling student, or having the courage to address lackluster data. According to Brown (2012), vulnerability can put us in a "torture chamber we call uncertainty" (p. 32). This is difficult to do on a good day, but can be especially hard when the person who will be critiquing our job performance is in the room.

As well intentioned as principals may be, they cannot divorce themselves from the critical role they play in the lives of teachers—the evaluator. And teachers know this. This is why it is hard to move beyond superficial collaboration. Teachers won't take risks, no matter how much they are encouraged to do so, if they are worried that their job performance is being critiqued or worse that their job is on the line. Growing up, how many of us shared confidences with teachers or favorite aunts before we did with our parents? We sought out these individuals because we needed a place to go and wrestle with an idea or dilemma; we needed some space to think and ask for advice. It was easier to be vulnerable with someone who didn't have the authority to take away the car keys. Rather than ignore this human dynamic, principals need to make sure that teachers have opportunities to wrestle with thorny issues and mess with the uncertainties of daily classroom decisions.

Learning Is Not a Linear Process

Learning is messy. It doesn't occur in a straight line that connects point A to point B. It is more akin to the two-step, where dancers take two steps forward and one step back. Deep learning requires time, practice, and feedback (Campitelli & Gobet, 2011). If this is the type of learning we want for teachers, then it is clear that traditional evaluation schemes won't get us there. Neither will the quick walk-throughs that provide little or no feedback. Teachers need feedback that helps form, shape, and mold effective practices into their classrooms. Leaders must regularly observe in classrooms and participate in collaborative discussions not so they can judge, but so they reflect and diagnose, helping teachers modify and adjust practices to more fully meet the needs of students. Supervision is a process; evaluation is an event. The summative nature of an evaluation can be helpful, but only when it is linked to the formative information gleaned through supervision practices (Marshall, 2013). It is the combination of both that helps teachers navigate the dance of learning.

Learning is also tricky because it doesn't happen in the same way, or at the same time, for everyone. Educators have long understood this as evidenced by the plethora of research and resources that promote differentiation in the classroom. Leaders need to understand that teachers aren't all starting at the same place or from the same vantage point when it comes to refining pedagogy. The type, frequency, and amount of observations and feedback need to be varied based on the needs of the teacher. Joyce and Showers's (1980) seminal work on professional development (PD) structures that result in deep levels of learning serves as the model for professional practices.

As people move from awareness to institutionalization, the types and structures of support must change. Figure 7.1 depicts the levels of support necessary. Support comes in layers rather than in tiers, an important distinction that results in multiple support structures depending on the desired level of impact. Teachers need opportunities to learn in large groups, small groups, and one-on-one. In other words, one size does not fit all, so a variety of structures must be utilized. Teachers need ample opportunities to learn in a variety of settings. This is one of the reasons why it is critical that the principal and the coach serve as partners in service of learning.

Figure 7.1 Professional Development Structures

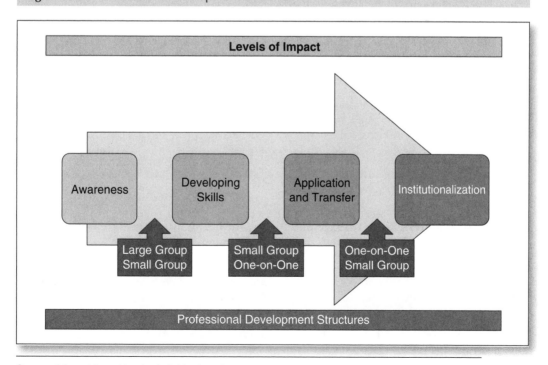

Source: Adapted from Mausbach & Morrison (2016).

Change Requires Pressure and Support

Fullan (2009) has taught us that whole system change requires a combination of high challenge (pressure) and high support (capacity building). Both the principal and coach play important, but distinct roles in providing this challenge and support. The coach's role is akin to the trusted aunt or teacher. They provide feedback and share their expertise. The principal creates structures and supports to promote learning and growth. They monitor progress through supervision practices that focus on ensuring quality instruction is in place for all children. Like coaches, they provide support, but they also have to ask tough questions and provide direct feedback so that all students in the school are getting what they need. Figure 7.2 outlines the subtle differences between what pressure and support look like from the vantage point of each role.

Figure 7.2 Behaviors of School Leader and Coach in Providing Pressure and Support

School Leader	Coach
Sets high expectations for teacher and student learning.	Provides support to teachers so they can meet the expectations that have been established by the school leadership.
Holds teachers accountable for meeting the needs of the students.	Organizes coaching so that it aligns with the accountability measures that are in place.
Establishes a vision and sets priorities for how to move student learning forward.	Prioritizes work that has the most potential to impact student learning.
Makes strategic use of the coach to move teacher learning forward.	Articulates the role of coach and engages teachers in the coaching process.
Leads the decision making about the scope and breadth of the content that is taught.	Helps teachers design instruction that aligns with expectations about the content that is taught.
Knows what high quality instruction looks like and sets the expectation that this is the norm throughout the school.	Skillfully supports teachers to implement high quality instruction.
Is aware of situations when students are underperforming and works to address the issue.	Works with teachers across all levels of performance.
Leads data-driven conversations with teachers and the coach.	Participates in data-driven conversations with teachers and the principal.
Spends time in classrooms and provides teachers with feedback as a result of the observations.	Spends time in classrooms to support the delivery of effective instruction.
Creates the structure and time for teachers to collaborate with each other and the coach.	Designs and facilitates collaboration among teachers.

Collective Teacher Efficacy Requires Self-Efficacy

Walk into some schools and you may see the banner, "TEAM: Together Everyone Achieves More." Given what we know about collective teacher efficacy those signs might need to be amended to read "TEAM: Together, When Everyone Believes, We Achieve More." Having a "together, we got this" attitude is what collective efficacy is about. Efficacy beliefs shape behaviors and actions. Staff with collective efficacy show greater effort and persistence, a willingness to try new approaches, and attend more closely to students who are struggling (Donohoo, 2017).

Getting to collective efficacy requires self-efficacy. Bandura (1997) defines teacher self-efficacy as "the conviction that one can successfully execute the behavior required to produce outcomes" (p. 193). When teachers believe they have the knowledge and skills to do the job, collaboration becomes more powerful. Without this conviction they may feel reluctant to share with others, or worse, feel that they would never be able to do what their colleagues are doing.

Collective teacher efficacy and self-efficacy are analogous to each other, and this makes sense. Our beliefs are shaped from our own experiences, but also from interacting with others. We need both to feel competent. Coaches create collective efficacy by helping individual teachers develop self-efficacy. Principals create collective efficacy by providing time, resources, and feedback to groups and individuals.

Assigning a coach to work with a struggling teacher sends a clear message to the teacher that they don't have what it takes to do the job, destroying any self-efficacy they might have developed. Telling teachers what they need to work on, the antithesis of student-centered coaching, erodes the collective efficacy of the school because it sends a signal to everyone that teachers need to be fixed. Knowing that collective teacher efficacy outranks every other factor in impacting student achievement, including socioeconomic status, prior achievement, home environment, and parental involvement (Hattie, 2015), it is just common sense to avoid any practice that undermines this critical element.

WHAT IT LOOKS LIKE

Two important things need to happen to ensure that coaches aren't a part of the supervision process. First, principals need to engage in effective supervision practices themselves. This includes aligning supervision to school improvement efforts by using differentiated supervision practices and knowing how to help struggling teachers. The second thing required is to understand and distinguish between the types of feedback that principals and coaches provide. The next sections will outline how we use effective supervision practices to support teacher development.

Leadership Move #1: Align Supervision to School Improvement

As outlined in Chapter 2, alignment of school improvement is when all the processes (mission and vision, data, the plan, PD and supervision) work in concert. Alignment is critical because it provides focus. Focus happens when what is of essential importance is identified and efforts are concentrated on these essentials. This focus is articulated in the school improvement plan and carried out in the PD plan. Professional development is the engine of school improvement, and supervision is the GPS (Mooney & Mausbach, 2008). Supervision provides guidance regarding how near or far a school is from its targets. The key for leaders is to make sure that they align the processes and help connect the dots for teachers. For example, if a strategy in the school improvement plan is implementing project-based learning, then the PD should focus on helping teachers use project-based learning. Individual professional growth plans would then include teachers identifying aspects of project-based learning that they are going to focus on throughout the year to improve their practice. Supervision is where the real work of implementing the school improvement plan happens. Without supervision the plan becomes another misguided initiative.

Leadership Move #2: Differentiate Supervision

Differentiated supervision means that school leaders do things differently based on what individual teachers need and what students deserve (Mooney & Mausbach, 2008). By matching the level of supervision with the needs and competencies of the individual, supervision is based on what the teacher actually needs rather than doing the same thing for everyone.

Keeping the coach out of the supervision process requires the school leader to have a clear pulse on the daily teaching and learning practices in the school. This can't happen if the leader is using a one-dimensional approach to supervision. While we are strong advocates for principals engaging in walk-throughs with feedback, that process alone won't provide a leader with the big picture needed to support and help staff grow. Differentiation by practice means using a variety of supervision methods to help understand the learning needs of the school so that appropriate supports can be provided (Mausbach & Morrison, 2016).

Figure 7.3 provides an outline of the differentiated practices that leaders can use. Leaders who have created a culture of learning in their schools understand that teachers need multiple opportunities to learn and grow, and a leader uses multiple methods to make this happen. While this can feel daunting, it can be done if a leader starts with the mindset that their number one job is to support teaching and learning in classrooms.

Figure 7.3 Differentiated Supervision Practices for School Leaders

Practice	Description	Purpose	Frequency	Feedback Method
General Walk-Through	Organized visit through a school's learning areas, using specific look fors to focus on teaching and learning. Observe for 3 minutes to 5 minutes per class	Identify building-wide trends and patterns regarding implementation of the school improvement plan to help determine next steps for professional learning	Daily	Face-to-face, schoolwide via blog, e-mail, principal newsletter
Focused Walk-Through	Observe teaching and learning in a specific grade level or content area Observe for 10 minutes to 20 minutes per class	Learn instructional strengths and needs of individual teachers Follow up on learning from team collaboration, such as professional learning communities (PLCs)	Depends on the work in small group PD, but on average it occurs with each teacher every 2 weeks	Face-to-face, e-mail, note
Implementation Study	Scheduled visits to measure quantitative data on implementation of the school improvement plan Time varies depending on the strategy	Determine how near or far the school is from reaching 100% implementation of strategies on the school improvement plan	Approximately 2 to 3 times per year	Schoolwide, face-to-face
Participation in Team Collaboration, such as PLCs	Weekly attendance at collaboration meetings to serve as an active team member	Play an active role in supporting teachers as they analyze student work and plan to meet the needs of all students	Attendance once a week per team	During meetings
Formal Evaluation	Process outlined by the school or district used to judge whether or not the teacher can continue to work at the school	Determine teacher competency	Annually or more frequently based on the needs of the teacher	Individualized

Source: Adapted from Mausbach & Morrison (2016).

Leadership Move #3: Work With Struggling Teachers

When it comes to working with teachers who are struggling, the saying "the best offense is a good defense" comes to mind. In other words, it is paramount when helping a struggling teacher to make sure that the principal has had ample opportunities to observe in the classroom prior to any formal interventions. Using differentiated practices helps the leader get a sense of the issues. A comprehensive view of the needs of a struggling teacher is necessary so that the leader can discern if formal evaluation processes need to be accessed. While formal evaluation systems can be poorly designed, they do provide guidance for the processes and procedures that should take place when a teacher is not making adequate progress.

Many coaches haven't had training on intensive support for teachers, nor should they. It is up to the principals to identify and implement necessary supports to help the teacher grow. Accessing the formal process communicates a message to the teacher that the intensity and frequency of the principal's supervision is shifting. Including the coach at this level is inappropriate because the shift moves from collaboration to a more directed and explicit approach.

Leadership Move #4: Don't Avoid Feedback—Just Use It Effectively

Leaders and coaches need to see and use feedback as a vehicle for growth. "Feedback is the fertilizer of professional learning. It helps nurture and accelerate growth" (Mausbach & Morrison, 2016, p. 55). Unfortunately in education, feedback has been viewed negatively due to its use or misuse with traditional teacher appraisal systems. The feedback associated with appraisals is predominantly evaluative in the sense that it is used to make judgements about how weak or strong a teacher or leader might be. We are advocating for the use of strengths-based feedback by both coaches and principals. Providing strengths-based feedback "enables us to engage with teachers in a way that honors the work they're doing while helping them growth as learners" (Sweeney & Harris, 2016, p. 118).

When discerning the difference between coach and principal feedback, think about the methods of a medical doctor versus a therapist. A medical doctor labels the issues and provides direct advice on what to do next (principal feedback), while the therapist listens, probes, and asks questions so the patient can discover answers (coaching feedback). Coaches need to focus on clarifying, valuing, and uncovering possibilities when providing feedback to teachers (Sweeney & Harris, 2016). Principals need to validate effective practices and help teachers refine and reflect on their methodology. Figure 7.4 provides examples of the differences in strengths-based feedback from the principal and coach perspective.

Figure 7.4 The Difference Between Principal and Coach Feedback

Principal Feedback Example	Coach Feedback Example
"When you shared the goal for the day, your students were confused. Turning your back to the class and changing your thinking about the goal led to this. Goals for the day need to be clear and explicit. Let's work on writing one together."	"During our coaching cycle we have been working on ensuring that the students understand the learning target for the day. How are the students doing with this?"
"Students seemed confused about the purpose for flagging information. They did not know what to flag. What type of thinking do you want students to be engaged in? How can you make that happen by teaching them to flag information in text?"	"Which specific students really understood how to flag text? Why did that seem to work for them?"
"There is a difference between asking, 'How did you solve it?' and 'What were you thinking?' When and how are you using these questions?"	"Let's take a look at how our students did when they were asked, 'How did you solve it?' versus 'What were you thinking?'"

LESSON FROM THE FIELD

Mark, an elementary school principal, met every Friday with his math and literacy coaches. They looked forward to taking time at the end of the week to monitor progress on their coaching cycles and reflect on next steps. To keep their conversations centered on their coaching goals, Mark used the same protocol each week. It had three steps: (1) coaches share data from coaching cycles, (2) coaches reflect on progress, and (3) the team brainstorms ideas for next steps based on the information that was shared. The protocol allowed the coaches to think aloud and provided rich context for their conversations.

One morning, Frank, the math coach, showed up early for the meeting. He was anxious to get started and asked to share what was happening in one of his coaching cycles. The goal of the cycle was to increase the students' use of questions during a math investigation. He knew that if students were going to engage in rich discourse, they needed to ask challenging and thought-provoking questions while they learned. The plan was to provide opportunities for students to construct viable arguments and critique the reasoning of others, yet little progress was being made. Frank admitted that he was at a loss for what to do next.

As the principal, Mark had been in the teacher's classroom on a weekly basis during walk-throughs. He was also at a loss for why this might be occurring. As they discussed the matter, Mark acknowledged that he needed to spend more time in the classroom so he could help Frank and the teacher identify what was getting in the way of helping the students engage in rigorous questioning. He advised Frank to continue the coaching cycle and let him know that he would step in as a leader as well. He assured Frank that this process wouldn't jeopardize the coach and teacher relationship because Mark spent time in classrooms on a regular basis as part of his overall supervision practices. Showing up and spending a little more time in the classroom wouldn't feel like something out of the norm because it wasn't.

The next week, Mark spent a few days in the teacher's classroom during the math block. He also reviewed the teacher's lesson plans. It became clear that while the learning targets were appropriate, the lesson wasn't being completed. The teacher was spending the majority of her time on the mini lesson, and students weren't getting to the investigation portion of the lesson. Mark concluded that the teacher was getting bogged down and needed to work on pacing.

Mark sat down with the teacher and narrated the lesson he had observed and compared it to her lesson plan. Through this discussion, the teacher began to understand that there was a discrepancy between what she had planned and her execution. This led to a discussion on how to pace a math workshop. They agreed on time frames for the segments of the lesson and decided that Mark would observe her next class with the sole focus of providing feedback on her pacing.

After the next observation, Mark shared what he saw, and the teacher was stunned. She had no idea her pacing was off. They decided that he would observe another lesson, and this observation resulted in a huge shift. This time, the teacher adjusted her instruction to allow more time for student discussion. Growth was happening.

While Mark was working with the teacher on her pacing, Frank continued with the coaching cycle. As a result of Mark's supervision, Frank noticed a significant shift. The teacher's deliberate attention to her pacing allowed her to provide the time the students needed to engage in rich discussion. This allowed them to work on the goals they had set for the coaching cycle.

Mark was grateful for the weekly meeting with the coaches because it helped him differentiate the supervision practices that he used with the teacher. Even though he had been in the classroom on a regular basis, he hadn't picked up on the nuances of the instructional issues that were occurring. Frank's ability to provide support and communicate the challenges allowed Mark to step in as the principal without ever putting Frank in an evaluative position.

The coach and principal partnership provided two layers of support that the teacher needed. Mark provided the first tier by helping the teacher manage instructional time through very directive feedback. The coach provided the second layer by helping students find their voice during math instruction. The teacher was supported by both her principal and coach. This combination of support helped make a real difference for students.

WHERE ARE YOU NOW?

There are some concrete things that principals can do to separate supervision from coaching. We suggest using the following rubric to self-assess and set goals around these important leadership moves (Figure 7.5).

Figure 7.5   Self-Assessment for School Leaders

Separate Coaching From Supervision			
	Accomplished	**Developing**	**Novice**
The School Leader	The school leader never asks the coach to engage in coaching that feels evaluative to teachers (i.e., walk-throughs, observations with checklists).	The school leader may ask the coach to engage in coaching that feels evaluative to teachers (i.e., walk-throughs, observations with checklists).	The school leader expects the coach to hold teachers accountable. This involves more evaluative coaching (i.e., walk-throughs, observations with checklists).
	The school leader uses coaching conversations to differentiate supervision practices.	Coaching conversations sometimes lead to evaluation.	The school leader uses coaching conversations to identify teachers who need to be on formal evaluation plans.
	The school leader uses differentiated supervision practices to get the pulse of the school.	The school leader uses one to two supervision practices infrequently and has a limited knowledge of the pulse of the school.	The school leader relies heavily on one supervision practice and has a limited knowledge of the pulse of the school.
Success Criteria	I can . . . • Support the coach to build trusting relationships with teachers • Build trusting relationships as the school principal • Avoid assigning coaching to people on improvement plans • Use differentiated supervision practices • Separate the coach from evaluative duties (i.e., walk-throughs, observations with checklists)		

Troubleshooting Around Separating Coaching From Supervision

It can be difficult for all members of the organization to understand why coaches should be separated from the supervision process. Well-intentioned district administrators might wonder why coaches aren't included in improvement plans for teachers. Teachers might prefer to work with a coach and wonder why the principal is spending so much time in their classroom. Figure 7.6 provides language to help principals navigate these conversations.

Figure 7.6 Language for Separating Coaching From Supervision

If I hear . . .	Then I can say . . .
"Why did we hire coaches if we aren't going to use them to help supervise teachers?"	"I understand why you would think that coaches should be involved in this process, especially given their rich content knowledge. However, it is critical that we keep them out of this process. A coach's role is to support not judge. We are asking our teachers to learn and try new things. No one likes to be judged when they are in the process of learning something new. We need to give our teachers an environment where they feel safe to grow. This can't happen if the coach is working from an evaluative stance."
"I have been working with a coach, why do I need to work with you?"	"I know the coach has been working with you on the specific goal of [insert student-centered coaching goal]. And I think that is great and that is going to continue. It has come to my attention through my walk-throughs and attendance at PLCs that there are some other areas where you need support."
"The reason you are putting pressure on me by coming into my classroom is because the coach is telling you that I am not doing a good job."	"I value my time in classrooms and during PLCs. This gives me a chance to have my own insights regarding teaching and learning throughout the schools. My insights are my own and not something the coach has reported to me."

THE COACH'S ROLE

Coaches have a responsibility to partner with the principal to ensure that their role does not become evaluative. This requires a coach to approach conversations with principals from a student-centered and strengths-based mindset. Centering discussions on the teacher rather than the students is a surefire way to march down the path toward evaluation. Coaches need to be clear about their role and avoid any behaviors that will misconstrue how they are perceived by their peers.

Avoid Replacement

Hidden agendas, mixed messages, and judgmental thinking are off limits if we want to ensure that coaching is nonevaluative. This may take some discipline because we are often tempted to focus on what should be replaced rather than on how to build on what's already there. Using this approach prevents the coach from getting traction because when teachers feel evaluated or judged they are far less likely to take a learning stance.

Three alternatives to "replacement" are (1) keep coaching focused on what the teacher would like to accomplish, (2) build on what's working, and (3) give the teacher time to learn and grow. You may be thinking, "What if nothing is working?" This is a great question and probably the one that leads us straight to a replacement mindset. So often, we want to fix things in spite of the fact that we aren't in charge of the classroom. It's a natural tendency because we want things to be better. Charlotte Danielson (2016) writes, "I'm deeply troubled by the transformation of teaching from a complex profession requiring nuanced judgment to the performance of certain behaviors that can be ticked off on a checklist" (p. 20). To honor this, we must take a deep breath and give learning the time that it requires. Teachers deserve coaching that navigates rather than circumvents the complexity within their classrooms.

Steer Clear of Walk-Throughs and Checklists

To put it bluntly, coaches shouldn't be involved in walk-throughs unless they are in the classroom working alongside a teacher when the walk-through occurs. Ask any teacher and he or she will tell you that walk-throughs are stressful situations. They worry about how they are being perceived, if they are doing things the correct way, and if the observers understand what is taking place in their classroom when the observation occurs. When a coach is part of the observation team, they take on an evaluative role. Here's a metaphor: When we watch a gymnastics meet there are judges on the sidelines. They look for the fundamentals of how a gymnast performs. They know what good gymnastics looks like and confirm or disconfirm if it is happening. This is a lot like a walk-through. Then there's the coach down on the mat with the gymnast. The coach is there to make sure that the athlete successfully reaches his or her goals. This is coaching. Separation of these roles is essential.

IN CLOSING

To create high performance schools, we need to attend to what teachers know and can do individually and collectively. In this way we can deliberately help them improve their practice over time (Hargreaves & Fullan, 2012). This is a monumental task that requires leaders to use resources strategically. Having coaches take on supervision and evaluation practices undermines their effectiveness and causes confusion. Separating coaches from supervision allows them to provide a space where teachers can be open to new learning and provide that deliberate practice needed for growth.

A gardener would never refer to their work as a plant business. While plants are essential to gardening, it is their development that matters. Instead of thinking "schools are a people business," let's switch our thinking to that of the gardener and understand that schools are a growth business. As leaders we need to create the best conditions for growth to occur. Keeping coaches out of supervision helps ensure that learning will take root, resulting in a bountiful harvest of student achievement.

8 Supporting the Development of the Coach

"I absolutely believe that people, unless coached, never reach their maximum potential."

—Bob Nardelli, CEO Home Depot

Lindsey Vonn is a world class ski racer who has won 77 World Cup races, an all-time women's record. She likes to go fast and rack up medals. It would be easy to think that her success is based on her innate skill (or lack of fear). But that is far from the truth. She is supported every step of the way. This helps her learn how to channel her skills in a way that gets her to the finish line first. Could you imagine if her coach said, "You've got this. We'll get out of your way and let us know if you need anything?" No way. Her coaches provide continuous feedback so that she isn't wondering where to put her effort. They steer her in the right direction so that she knows how she might focus on her fitness, her race technique, and her diet.

Nobody assumes that "Lindsey's got this." Yet this is how so many school leaders approach their instructional coaches. They hire the best teachers to become coaches and then leave them alone. Coaching is far too important to take this approach.

WHY IT MATTERS

Adult Learning Is Different Than Student Learning

Sweeney (2011) writes,

> Any coach will tell you that the shift from teaching to coaching is dramatic. Some coaches are lonely and miss the close connection they had with students. Others are in roles that are poorly articulated. Some are not prepared for working with adult learners. Others may face school cultures that are downright hostile to coaching. To meet these challenges, coaches require ongoing support. (p. 161)

Make no bones about it, working with adult learners is multifaceted and demanding. Coaches need tremendous support if they are going to make the impact we are looking for. This support may come from school administrators, district level leaders, or both. Wherever it comes from, it is essential for every coaching program. In the article, *Pave the Way for Coaches*, Heineke and Polnick (2013) write, "As administrators step up to the plate and provide support for instructional coaching, they will ensure that the money and time invested in professional learning will pay off with greater dividends in sustained teacher growth and student achievement" (p. 51).

We must help coaches develop their skills in working with adult learners. As a leader in adult development, Jane Vela (2002) provides 12 principles to guide us (Figure 8.1). As you read the principles, be prepared to be overwhelmed. There are so many factors, and each one is equally as complex as the next.

If coaches are going to meet these demands, they need to be versed not only in content skills, but also in "soft" skills as well. Soft skills encompass the ability to get along well with others and include effective listening, relationship building, practicing empathy, social intelligence, being a learner, and having a positive attitude. It's simply not enough to help with the craft of coaching because there are so many factors on the table. Coaches need to understand how to help teachers process new information, how to own the content that they are learning, and how to make decisions that are grounded in what's best for the students. It's up to the principal to make sure they hone these skills.

Coaches Need a Predictable Structure

Given how precious coaching is, it would be silly to neglect such a resource. A key strategy to support coaches is to provide them with

Figure 8.1 Vela's Principles of Working With Adult Learners

- *Needs assessment:* Learners name what is to be learned
- *Safety:* Learners trust the environment and the process
- *Sound relationships:* Between and among learners
- *Sequence of content*: Learning follows a logical flow
- *Praxis:* Learning by doing
- *Respect:* Learners are treated as decision makers
- *Ideas, feelings, and actions:* Cognitive, affective, and psychomotor aspects of learning are addressed
- *Immediacy:* Learning is applied quickly
- *Clear roles:* Roles are developed thoughtfully
- *Teamwork:* Learners participate in small group collaboration
- *Engagement:* Learning is meaningful
- *Accountability:* Learners articulate how they know what they know

Source: Adapted from Vela, J. (2002). *Learning to Listen, Learning to Teach: The Power of Dialogue in Educating Adults* (p. 4). San Francisco, CA: Jossey-Bass.

a predictable structure. This establishes a clear path to follow, which in turn increases the impact they will make on student and teacher learning. Goodwin (2013) writes,

Coaching can fall flat if coaches lack a structured approach. A study of an initiative that provided loosely structured peer coaching for mathematics teachers, for example, found no positive effects on student achievement; the researchers noted that coaching conversations tended to be superficial and non-confrontational, providing little real guidance to teachers.

Providing structure includes defining the steps involved in a coaching cycle, setting up processes for collaboration, framing expectations for teacher participation in coaching, and providing regular opportunities for the coach to receive feedback from the school leader. Each of these steps establishes a clear path for the coach to follow and ensures that coaching doesn't become too informal.

Unfocused Evaluation of Coaches Is Worthless

More often than not, it seems that coaches are an afterthought when a district negotiates the plan for their evaluation. Applying a criterion that is meant for teachers doesn't fit the day-to-day work of a coach. Danielson and McGreal (2000) write, "A single set of evaluative criteria is unlikely to be suitable to all those individuals in a school who are included in the teachers' contract. They are typically written with the classroom teacher in mind" (p. 38).

The evaluation tool matters, and so does the process. Some districts try to address this challenge by using an evaluation that is designed for "specialists." This is a catch-all for staff members such as reading specialists, curriculum developers, library media teachers, English as a second language teachers, and so on. These criteria are too generic and often miss the expectations that we have for coaches. It's an exercise in futility to spend precious time evaluating a coach with a tool that doesn't really describe his or her work. Later in this chapter we detail the process a principal might use to evaluate a coach using a framework that is based on the practices for student-centered coaching.

Keep Your Eye on Impact

A resource as important as coaching demands program evaluation. Continuous evaluation of the coaching program leads to greater impact overall. It also supports the development of the coach because nothing is left to chance. The pulse of teachers is taken, data is analyzed, and learning is monitored. Otherwise, why are we here?

It can be helpful to think about Guskey's (2002) five levels of evaluation as signposts for evaluating the impact of a coaching effort (p. 45). Figure 8.2 details these levels in relation to student-centered coaching. We recommend for principals and coaches to use these levels to discuss the impact of coaching at least twice a year. In this way, the program will continue to evolve, the coach will be supported, and students will be served.

WHAT IT LOOKS LIKE

The best person to provide feedback to the coach is the person sitting in the principal's office. The reason for this is that the school leader understands the complexities of the school and is the person who is ultimately responsible for what happens. We can never underestimate how much feedback a coach needs. If the only feedback a coach receives is from a coach meeting or rare visit from a district leader, then it's probably not enough. Supporting a coach is a continuous conversation in which the principal and coach engage as partners to move the school toward the goal. This takes intention and a plan.

Figure 8.2 Guskey's Five Levels of Evaluation

Level	Focus of the Principal and Coach Conversation
1. Teachers' Reactions	This information is gathered by coaches at the end of their coaching cycles: • *How do the teachers feel about student-centered coaching?* • *What do they believe were the benefits of participating in a coaching cycle?* • *Do teachers have any feedback for making coaching more beneficial?*
2. Teachers' Learning	This information is based on coaches' reflection and analysis of coaching cycles: • *Did the teachers learn to implement new instructional practices during a coaching cycle?* • *Did the coaching cycle focus on a goal that the teachers set for their own growth and development?* • *If learning didn't occur, why?*
3. School Culture	This information is based on principal and coach analysis of the coaching program: • *Was coaching supported by the administration?* • *Were there adequate resources allocated?* • *Was success of teachers and students recognized and shared?*
4. Teachers' Use of New Knowledge and Skills	This information is gathered from teachers who have participated in coaching: • *Was the teacher able to apply the new learning that was garnered during the coaching cycle?* • *Did the teacher apply the learning to other subjects or contexts?* • *Did the coach follow up with the teacher after the coaching cycle had ended?*
5. Student Learning Outcomes	This information is based on the data collected across the coaching cycle: • *What was the impact on students during the coaching cycle?* • *Are the students more confident as learners now that the cycle is complete?* • *Are the students able to demonstrate their performance both formatively and summatively?*

Source: Adapted from Guskey, T. (2002). Does it make a difference? Evaluating professional development. *Educational Leadership, 71*(2), 78–80.

Leadership Move #1: Support Coaches to Build Relationships

Relationships are the foundation of coaching. If coaches struggle to build relationships, then they won't make it to the finish line. One way coaches can do this is to vigorously embody an attitude of openness and curiosity. James Flaherty (1999), a preeminent voice in coaching, addresses this when he writes, "Coaching is a learning experience for both the coach and client. Unless we question our assumptions, abandon our techniques, and vigilantly correct the outcomes we're producing, we will soon fail as coaches" (p. 12). For some, this comes easily. For others, it can be more of a struggle.

But even with the importance of relationships, we can't allow coaches to get stuck in the relationship-building stage forever. This will cause a coach to become too passive, and the coaching work will be diminished. We also have to ensure that coaches don't come on too strong and offend teachers. This may cause the coach to become isolated within the school community. When this is the case, the leader must help the coach correct the behavior before too much damage is done. While it can be touchy to discuss interpersonal relationships, a savvy principal can provide tremendous support by helping the coach take thoughtful steps to build and sustain relationships with all members of the school community.

For example, a principal might shadow a coach to collect data regarding how a coach is engaging in reflective dialogue with teachers. Then the principal would provide the coach with real-time feedback about their conversational discourse. Another strategy is to use the Rubric for Student-Centered Coaching (Appendix B) to have concrete conversations with coaches that are built on a success criterion for coaching. Finally, there is always the option of using video as a tool for recording and reflecting on coaching conversations. While video can be intimidating, it is quite powerful for a principal and coach to break down a conversation using a play-by-play format to develop the coach's ability to foster trust and respect when working with teachers.

Leadership Move #2: Carefully Plan Your Principal and Coach Meetings

Principal and coach meetings occur weekly or biweekly and are an opportunity to get on the same page with the coach. We've noticed that although some principals and coaches meet regularly, they may be discussing the wrong things. Many principal and coach meetings focus on the activities that the coach is engaging in with teachers, such as which professional development (PD) structures are being used and with whom. In essence, it feels like a calendar review rather than a conversation about impact. We believe that if we are going to drive toward improving teaching and learning, then principal and coach meetings ought to focus on the growth that they are seeing in classrooms.

When working with a team of coaches last year, Diane asked the group to record planning conversations that they were having with the principal and assistant principal. Then they watched the videos and looked for patterns. One of the conversations stood out from the rest. Amanda was struck by the fact that she and her principal didn't spend any time discussing student learning. Instead, they talked at length about all the things that were going on in the school.

Amanda went back to school and suggested that they rethink their principal and coach meetings. This involved creating a simple agenda to use each week. This way they would have a well-thought-out plan and would stay focused on the right things (Figure 8.3). This year, Amanda works in two schools and continues to use this structure when she meets with the administrators in both. They value the structure and find their planning time to be highly beneficial.

It's important to note that discussing the impact of coaching demands a certain level of transparency, especially if we hope to monitor how coaching is impacting student and teacher learning. Keeping coaching confidential undermines the partnerships that we are trying to build. This doesn't mean that the principal and coach hide behind a closed door and criticize teachers. Rather, conversations are framed around continuous growth. We are all here to learn, and monitoring how we are doing is tremendously important.

Figure 8.3 Agenda for Weekly Principal and Coach Meeting

1. **Review of Coaching Cycles (past, current, or future)—8 minutes**

   - *This part of the conversation is a quick recap so the principal gets an overall picture of the coach's work and reviews goals for student learning.*

2. **Discuss Trends That the Principal Is Seeing—12 minutes**

   - *This is not specific to teachers and isn't about evaluation data. Rather, it is a discussion of general trends that the principal has noticed while in classrooms and during teacher collaboration. This focuses on instructional practice and student learning.*

3. **Planning and Next Steps—12 minutes**

   - *Plan future PD, discuss how teachers who are engaged in coaching will be celebrated, and identify how the principal can continue to support the coaching effort.*
   - *Identify upcoming opportunities for the principal to shadow the coach.*

Leadership Move #3: Be a Part of the Coach's Work

Principals' lives are busy. This busyness may tempt a principal to delegate teacher development to the coach, especially if the coach is competent and capable. There is so much pressure to improve teaching and learning, and here is a dedicated person to do just that. Now the principal can focus on everything else. This is a mistake. It is critical for principals to find the time to be a part of the coach's work. Teacher development is too important to outsource. Outsourcing also sends a message that coaching isn't a priority because the principal can't find the time to be a part of it. If the principal is never observing the coach in action, then they can't identify what the coach needs to improve on.

One way a principal can stay involved in the coaching is through short, frequent, and focused observations. This sets the stage for the principal to understand the work that is taking place; it also sets the principal up to provide needs-based support to the coach. Observations can focus on any aspect of coaching, such as goal-setting sessions, unpacking learning targets, co-planning, co-teaching, or collaborations like professional learning communities or learning teams. Let's say a coach is in the last few days of a coaching cycle, the principal may choose to join the teacher and coach as they discuss the growth of the students. What a strong message this sends. It shows that the principal is aware of the work the teachers are doing with the coach, that the principal cares, and that growth is being celebrated.

Whenever we encourage principals to join in coaching conversations, we remind them to maintain a positive stance. It is tempting in these situations to shift into a deficit mindset about teachers. It may be that the classroom was a bit chaotic. Or that the teacher wasn't entirely clear during the instruction. The principal may be thinking, "Haven't we talked about this before? Why is this teacher still struggling?" It's vital for the principal to set those concerns aside for the moment and focus on the coaching. There will be plenty of time for the coach to help the teacher get better. We may think we are savvy at hiding our negative feelings, but we'd argue that they leak out. Mostly because the teachers' antennas are always up and listening for evaluation or judgment. Later, the principal and coach can more generally discuss the gaps that they are noticing throughout the school and make a plan for how those gaps will be addressed. Learning takes time, and this is important to keep in mind.

Leadership Move #4: Provide the Coach With Strengths-Based Feedback

Many coaches are like Lindsey Vonn. They are elite athletes who work tirelessly to do their job well. They are their own worst critics, and they crave feedback. For this reason, coaches need coaching. This may come from the principal, a district leader, or both. Providing the coach with feedback doesn't have to be overwhelming or take a lot of time. The key is that it helps the coach understand how to grow as a practitioner.

Observations are followed by feedback that is strengths-based. Strengths-based feedback is informed by the work of Cheliotes and Reilly. In their book, *Coaching Conversations: Transforming Your School One Conversation at a Time*, they suggest a framework for providing what they call "reflective feedback" using the following steps:

1. Clarifying questions or statements

2. Value statements or questions

3. Questions or possibility statements (Cheliotes & Reilly, 2010, p. 67)

Later in this chapter, we have included a Lesson From the Field that shares how a principal used strengths-based feedback to support the development of her (highly skilled) coach. Having been a coach herself, she understands how important it is to carve out time for these conversations.

Leadership Move #5: Evaluate Coaches With the Right Tool

If we hope to provide support to coaches, then we need tools. One of the most high leverage tools for reinforcing the practices for student-centered coaching is an aligned evaluation tool. Using a tool that isn't aligned with the coach's work is a disservice to the coach and the person who is spending precious time on the evaluation itself. The Rubric for Student-Centered Coaching features seven traits that we consider to be essential qualities for coaches. These traits are a useful guide for supporting the development of a coach (Figure 8.4). The full rubric can be found in Appendix B.

Building an evaluation system around these coaching moves aligns evaluation with the practices that we hope coaches will use on a consistent basis. It also captures the complexity of being an effective coach and therefore gives coaches room to develop and grow.

The Rubric for Student-Centered Coaching uses the same format as the self-assessments that are included for principals throughout this book. There are descriptors of what it looks like when a coach is novice, developing, and accomplished. There is also a success criteria featuring concrete look fors that are written as "I can" statements.

Districts can build a yearlong plan for using the rubric as the evaluation tool. For example, at the beginning of the year, coaches set a goal based on the rubric. Then the coaches' supervisor (principal or district

Figure 8.4 Qualities of Effective Coaches

1. The coach understands and implements the core practices for student-centered coaching.

2. The coach designs systems and structures to engage teachers in coaching cycles.

3. The coach understands effective instruction and helps teachers implement it.

4. The coach builds trusting and respectful relationships with teachers.

5. The coach provides skilled facilitation during collaboration and professional learning.

6. The coach maintains a learning stance.

7. The coach engages in reflective dialogue with teachers.

leader) engages in focused observations to see the coach in action and provide feedback. At the end of the school year, coaches are more formally observed and provide the evaluator with data from their coaching cycles. With this information at the table, the principal and coach are prepared to have specific conversations around how to continue to develop the skills of the coach.

The hope for any evaluation process is for good work to be highlighted and celebrated and for those who are struggling to receive more intensive support. This process accomplishes both of these objectives.

LESSON FROM THE FIELD

As a 3rd-year principal in a large comprehensive high school, Shawn wanted to do a better job supporting her coach. She had been a coach in her previous role and knew how lonely the job could be. She felt that she had dropped the ball in the previous year due to the tragic loss of a student, and this year Shawn planned to step up her support to the coach.

In August, she invited her coach to discuss a plan of support. Kelly was resilient and was used to operating on her own, so when her principal asked her how she could provide more support, Kelly was unsure. Shawn said, "The principal team is implementing mini-observations. I wonder if I could use that strategy with you as well." Shawn added, "We are learning that short and much more frequent observations can be more effective than fewer, longer ones. What if we put a monthly observation on our calendars? You could choose what I'd observe and provide me with a focus? Then we'd chat afterward."

Kelly liked the idea. They chose the first observation to be of Kelly working with a science teacher. For the previous few months, the school had been working on using technology to formatively assess students. While this coaching cycle integrated technology, it was primarily focused on a unit covering metabolic processes. They were also working on how to develop lessons that were more engaging.

As the observation began, Shawn joined Kelly and the teacher as they sat down together. Earlier in the day, they had taught a lesson on enzymes. At the end of the lesson, the students used technology to complete a formative assessment to check their understanding. This would be the student evidence that they would be examining. Just to be sure that the teacher wasn't intimidated by her participation, Shawn explained that she was there to learn more about how coaching was going in the school.

As the conversation got going, Kelly and the teacher began analyzing the student work based on the learning targets that related to the function and structure of enzymes. Since the students had completed the assessment electronically, Kelly had made copies of their responses and brought three different colors of highlighters so they could mark them based on if they got it, were close, or were far away from what the teacher was looking for. This information would then inform the next lesson. As they moved through the process, it took longer than expected. As a result, they didn't have time to plan the next lesson. The teacher didn't seem to mind continuing their conversation after school, so that's what they agreed to do.

After the coaching session, Shawn and Kelly met to discuss how it went. Shawn used the process for strengths-based feedback, and their conversation sounded like this (Figure 8.5).

Figure 8.5 Providing a Coach with Strengths-Based Feedback

Shawn Begins by Clarifying

Shawn: When we set up the observation you mentioned that the teacher wanted help planning her lessons. Can you tell me a bit more about that?

Kelly: We agreed that planning together might help. She's getting behind the rest of her team, and she has some pretty complex content to teach. She's trying to use PowerPoint slides to stay focused, but the kids get her off track. It's been frustrating for her, so she asked for my help.

Shawn: How did it go when you met after school?

Kelly: It went well. We planned out the next lesson and how she will teach it. I think it will be a nice extension based on our analysis of the student work. We are moving away from slides and helping her design some more engaging learning by using technology.

(Continued)

(Continued)

Shawn:	Can you tell me a little bit about how you structured the planning?
Kelly:	Sure. I used a Planner for Sharing Lessons (see Appendix F). It helped us chunk the lesson and make sure that the students would be doing something to process the information that she was sharing. We also co-planned our roles for how it will be taught. My role was to collect student evidence, while the students were engaged in the learning. She took on the teaching.

Shawn Values What She Saw

Shawn:	I'm glad you are finding tools that work for you. This was important to me when I was a coach. I think it helps teachers feel like they are in good hands and that we aren't winging it.
Kelly:	Thanks, I like to share the tools with teachers as well. This way we are both on the same page.
Shawn:	That's great.

Shawn and Kelly Uncover Possibilities

Kelly:	The only thing that bothered me was the fact that we ran out of time. This happens to me a lot, and I hate to ask her to finish after school.
Shawn:	Interesting. I wonder if there are more streamlined ways to analyze the student work so that you have more time for planning.
Kelly:	Any thoughts?
Shawn:	Well, as I listened, I noticed that you lost focus a few times. It was a good discussion, but you spent significant time talking at length about specific students. These are students who are tricky, and the teacher seemed to be looking for help from you. While this is important, it took away from the analysis of the formative assessments and the planning that you hoped to do.
Kelly:	That's true. We did lose focus a few times. I could work on that.
Shawn:	Maybe you could create some kind of virtual parking lot where you put these concerns and then follow up on them later.
Kelly:	I can do that. My plan was to focus on the assessment from today, but the teacher seemed to want to discuss the students in broader generalities. That threw me off.
Shawn:	That could be addressed through a simple purpose statement at the beginning of the session. Something like, "We are here to talk through the formative assessments from yesterday so we can plan the next lesson. If we have other concerns, let's save them for the end."
Kelly:	Great idea. I always take these kinds of things for granted. I need to frame things more clearly.
Shawn:	It sounds like you learned a few things today. I'm excited that you are partnering with this teacher, and it seems like she really values working with you. What are your next steps?
Kelly:	I'm going to try creating a parking lot in the Google Doc where we take notes. I think this will work with another teacher I'm working with, too. I'm also going to frame the purpose before every conversation. Thanks, this has really helped me.

As you read this conversation, you may have noticed that it felt natural while also providing specific feedback. Shawn avoided the dreaded question of, "How do you think it went?" A surefire way to make Kelly feel anxious and defensive. Instead she began with what Kelly had named as her goal with the teacher. Shawn also encouraged Kelly to decide which of the next steps she would try. This grounded the conversation in her own work and allowed her to take ownership throughout.

WHERE ARE YOU NOW?

The following assessment creates the opportunity for school leaders to reflect on the support they are providing to a coach. This rubric could also be useful to district leaders who are leading a coaching effort. Schools have different structures regarding who supervises a coach. Think flexibly and plan how the assessment might be used.

Figure 8.6 Self-Assessment for School Leaders

Support the Coach to Develop as a Practitioner			
	Accomplished	**Developing**	**Novice**
The School Leader	The school or district leader understands and supports the implementation of student-centered coaching. Time is allocated for the coach and principal to meet on a regular basis. The coach receives feedback regarding how coaching is going. Evaluation of coaching is aligned with the core practices for student-centered coaching.	The school or district is developing an understanding of student-centered coaching. The principal and coach meet informally to touch base, and support for the coach is less predictable and consistent. Evaluation of coaching is generic and doesn't identify student-centered coaching practices.	The school or district is developing an understanding of student-centered coaching. The principal and coach do not meet together or work collaboratively. Evaluation of coaching is not aligned with the core practices for student-centered coaching.
Success Criteria	I can . . . ● Meet with the coach on a regular basis (weekly or biweekly) and ask open-ended questions about his or her coaching work ● Create conditions where the coach feels comfortable taking a learning stance ● Evaluate the impact of the coaching program with an aligned framework ● Observe the coach on a regular basis ● Provide strengths-based feedback to the coach ● Evaluate the coach using the Rubric for Student-Centered Coaching			

Troubleshooting Around Supporting Coaches

It can be easy to have the best intentions regarding supporting a coach to develop. Then with the reality of life in schools, time becomes scarce and this becomes the first thing to go. We'd advocate that since well-positioned and well-trained coaches have the ability to make such an impact on teaching and learning, then they should be prioritized. The following scenarios provide language for the times when this prioritization is challenged (Figure 8.7).

THE COACH'S ROLE

Asking for help (and feedback) may be the first step for a coach. We are often guilty of putting our heads down and powering through difficult situations. This is a less-than-productive way to grow and develop. If there isn't an established time for principal and coach meetings, then request to meet. If there are meetings occurring but they aren't structured, suggest an agenda. If you aren't receiving feedback, then help the principal understand what would support you the most. The principal and coach relationship is truly a partnership. Advocate for what you need using the following strategies.

Figure 8.7   Language for Supporting Coaches

If I hear . . .	Then I can say . . .
[The coach] says, "I think I'll go back to the classroom. Coaching isn't what I thought it would be."	"It can be an adjustment to go from teacher to coach. Let's create a plan that will increase the support you're receiving. We can tighten up our principal and coach meetings, and I'll sit in during your sessions so that I can provide you with reflective feedback. We can also partner you up with a mentor coach who will help you problem solve challenges that you are facing."
[The coach] says, "I know you are busy. I think I have this coaching thing handled."	"I know you have a very strong skill set, but remember how we believe in a growth mindset here. We can all always use support to do our jobs. Let's create a plan that helps you continue to grow."
[A teacher] says, "I hope that the coach doesn't run and tell the principal about all the things that I need to improve. I know they meet together, and it makes me nervous."	"The coach and teacher relationship is built on trust, so I don't probe the coach about how teachers are doing. I'd rather find that out by myself by spending time in classrooms. When the coach and I meet, we discuss how to keep the school moving forward as a learning community."

Be Open to Learning

Taking the stance of expert backfires every time. Rather, coaches who consistently seek opportunities for learning are more effective. Is it okay for a coach to lean in and provide guidance? Sure. But that's different than taking on the mantle of telling teachers what to do and how to do it.

Most coaches are expected to work beyond their grade level or content area. In these cases, it's even more important to take the stance of learner. Otherwise, teachers will call the coach's bluff and the coach will lose credibility. Being viewed as a "master teacher" may also hinder a coach's ability to advocate for his or her own growth. There is no better way for coaches to send the message that learning is essential than by learning themselves. One way coaches can do this is to share how they are learning and growing. This habit serves as a connector between coaches, teachers, and the school leader. It's about transparency, and transparency is about learning. We are all learners, and we all need to maintain a learning stance.

Set Goals That Focus on One Thing at a Time

If we had a dollar for every time a coach asked, "Am I doing it right?" While we appreciate the commitment of these coaches, we find ourselves reminding them that coaching is complex and challenging work. Remember Figure 8.1, Vela's principles for adult learning? They remind us that supporting adult learning is multidimensional.

Instead of thinking of it as right or wrong, we suggest for coaches to prioritize their own plan for improvement and then work that plan. The Rubric for Student-Centered Coaching is a comprehensive look at what student-centered coaching looks like when it's done well. It can be instrumental for coaches to use the rubric to track their own development. We'd caution against trying to do it all at once, because it's just too much. It's far more effective for coaches to work in partnership with their principal to set incremental goals for their own development, thus focusing on one aspect of coaching at a time. When this approach is taken, then the coach will be able to feel the progress that is happening in their day-to-day coaching work.

Be Honest With the Principal

There's nothing worse than feeling overwhelmed and not having anyone to go to for help. We've said it before: Coaching can be a lonely job considering the fact that it is a unique role. Throughout this chapter, we've identified a variety of ways that a principal and coach can work together in the pursuit of personal development. The key is that we understand that charting a path for our own growth is rooted in embracing our vulnerability. We have to be able to identify where we are struggling and seek help from the school leader. This can be scary because when coaches are hired, they often believe that they have to have it all figured out. This false notion is based on the idea that coaching is straightforward and easy. It will never be straightforward and easy. That's what makes it so much fun. Name your challenges and work through them with the principal. Faking it doesn't get us anywhere.

IN CLOSING

Supporting coaches (and a coaching effort) can be challenging. It demands a vision that meets the requirements of the system while also addressing the needs of the individual coach. What we can't do is assume that coaches are smart people who can figure it out on their own. Taking this approach puts coaches in a lonely position and can disrupt the entire coaching model.

There are so many facets to supporting a coach. It is provided through high quality, or strengths-based, feedback. It is provided through aligned and thoughtful evaluation. It is provided through regularly scheduled and purposeful meetings. None of this is random and spontaneous. It is all planned in advance, and in this way, nobody is left to fall through the cracks. We are all learners, and we all need feedback. If we treat our coaches like precious Olympians and provide them with coaching and support, then we will get much more out of the coaching effort.

In Closing

"What we want for our children . . . we should want for their teachers;
that schools be places of learning for both of them, and that such learn-
ing be suffused with excitement, engagement, passion, challenge, cre-
ativity, and joy."

—Andy Hargreaves

While reading this book, a voice in the back of your mind may have been whispering, "But my teachers are overwhelmed. There is so much to do. How could I possibly pull this off?" Our answer is that this work is never going to be easy, but it can be less hard, especially when we build strong partnerships.

So much of this book is focused on clarity. Clarity around what coaching looks like. Clarity around school improvement and high quality instruction. Clarity around the coaching role, how teachers are expected to engage in coaching, and the importance of separating coaching from supervision. And clarity around creating a culture that embraces coaching and supports the development of the coach. We've focused on these areas because when you find clarity, everything falls into place. Schools become more joyful, instruction becomes more precise, teachers are happier, and students learn.

As leaders we sometimes feel that we have to be strong and all knowing, when in reality leading is mired in uncertainty and ambiguity. Being unsure of ourselves is natural, and the mark of a great leader is when we aren't afraid to admit that and seek help from those around us. If you are reading this book, and are lucky enough to have a coach, don't squander this most valuable resource. The coach can be just the person to help you be the leader that you want to be.

Knowing how much you want to get done, remember that every journey starts with one small step. It isn't a matter of doing it all at once, it is about starting somewhere. It would be great if this was a linear process, but it isn't. The starting point for each school is different. Don't forget that your coach is one of your most valuable assets. Engage in conversations to determine what is working and what isn't. Then go from there.

No matter where you start, remember that the purpose for school is student learning. If you keep this in mind, then you are in a much better position to design teacher support that impacts student achievement. This can be challenging because it may feel as if there is a magnet pulling you away from what matters most. What can draw you back are the relationships you develop throughout the school, particularly with your coach. Nobody needs to be isolated. Not the principal, the coach, the teachers, or the students. This gets at the heart of student-centered coaching. If we work together to accomplish our goals for learning, then we'll create the schools that we want for our teachers and students.

Appendix A

*Rubric for Leading
Student-Centered Coaching*

Effective Principals:

1. Understand the philosophy and methods for student-centered coaching
2. Develop systems for professional learning and coaching
3. Clearly define the coach's role
4. Create a culture of learning
5. Set expectations for authentic participation in coaching
6. Understand pedagogy and curricular content
7. Separate coaching from supervision
8. Support the coach to develop as a practitioner

Understand the Philosophy and Methods for Student-Centered Coaching			
	Accomplished	**Developing**	**Novice**
The School Leader	The principal understands the core practices for student-centered coaching, subscribes to these practices, and provides support to move coaching forward.	The principal has some knowledge of the core practices for student-centered coaching, may question its value, or may not be actively involved in the coaching effort.	The principal is not supportive of, lacks knowledge in, or takes a passive approach to supporting the implementation of the core practices for student-centered coaching.

(Continued)

(Continued)

Understand the Philosophy and Methods for Student-Centered Coaching			
	Accomplished	**Developing**	**Novice**
	The principal provides the necessary pressure and support to ensure that coaching is used to its full potential.	The principal is beginning to find a balance between providing the adequate pressure and support to ensure that coaching is used to its full potential.	The principal focuses on either pressure or support rather than finding a balance between the two. Coaching is not used to its full potential.
Success Criteria	I can . . . • Support the coach to effectively use the core practices for student-centered coaching • Organize the schedule make time for coaching to occur • Facilitate data collection and use data in collaborations, such as PLCs • Create the infrastructure for regular data analysis • Avoid using coaching in a punitive manner • Supervise and support teachers who are at risk rather than asking the coach to do so		

Develop Systems for Professional Learning and Coaching			
	Accomplished	**Developing**	**Novice**
The School Leader	The school leader aligns professional development (PD) and coaching to schoolwide goals and initiatives. This creates a focus for teacher development and student learning. There is a well-designed PD plan that includes large group, teacher teams, and individualized support for teachers.	The school leader is working to establish a focus for teacher development and student learning. The school leader may be challenged to prioritize or stay the course with the school improvement effort. The PD plan isn't used to its full potential. It lacks connections between large group, teacher teams, and individualized support for teachers.	The school leader doesn't create a PD plan that is executed on. This creates an unfocused professional development environment. There are many topics covered when it comes to PD. There aren't connections made between large group, teacher teams, and individualized support for teachers.
Success Criteria	I can . . . • Work with the coach and teacher leaders to create a student-centered school improvement plan (SIP) and PD plan • Execute the plan by revisiting it during the principal and coach meetings • Use data to guide SIP, PD, and coaching • Make connections between large group, teacher teams, and individualized support for teachers • Listen and adapt the plan based on student performance and teacher feedback		

Clearly Define the Coach's Role			
	Accomplished	**Developing**	**Novice**
The School Leader	Works with the coach to define what coaching is about. The coach's role is then publicized to the broader school community. It is also revisited throughout the year to encourage teacher participation and reinforce how the coach is positioned to impact student and teacher learning.	Attempts to define the role of the coach, but there may be things on the coach's list of duties that pull him or her away from coaching. Or, as the year progresses, the role of the coach isn't maintained. Teachers have an uneven vision of the coach's role, or why there is a coach in the school.	Defers to others to define the coach's role. "Others" may be district leadership, the coach, or fate. The coach's role isn't publicized, and teachers do not have a shared vision of why there is a coach in the school.
Success Criteria	I can . . . • Reflect with my coach using a Venn diagram to determine how the principal and coach's roles overlap and are distinct • Guard the coach's role and responsibilities • Support the coach to build systems and structures that align with his or her role • Work with the coach to develop a communications plan to publicize the coach's role • Continually reinforce the importance of coaching as well as the role of the coach • Delegate busy work to other staff members		

Create a Culture of Learning			
	Accomplished	**Developing**	**Novice**
The School Leader	A culture of learning is created, thus creating the conditions for teachers to engage authentically in coaching cycles and other PD. The school leader sets the tone that "we are all learners" and models this behavior throughout all interactions with teachers.	The school lacks a growth mindset among teachers. Thus there are pockets where a culture of learning is beginning, but there is room for improvement. The school leader is working toward developing transparency regarding his or her own learning and development.	The school leader reinforces a more privatized school culture in which teachers hunker down and avoid coaching. There is a lack of trust among teachers.
Success Criteria	I can . . . • Build a positive culture around coaching • Model having a growth mindset • Make my learning transparent • Take risks as a learner • Listen to teachers and ask open-ended questions		

Set Expectations for Authentic Participation in Coaching

	Accomplished	Developing	Novice
The School Leader	The principal frames coaching as being for all teachers because all teachers have students with needs. The school leader encourages teachers to engage in coaching cycles and celebrates growth that occurs as a result of cycles.	The principal frames coaching cycles as either "mandated" or "invitational." As a result, some teachers participate authentically, some choose to opt-out, and others may participate in a compliance-driven fashion.	The principal leaves it up to the coach to set expectations for participation in coaching cycles. Teachers view coaching as something that doesn't really include or affect them. Certain teachers participate and others steer clear.
Success Criteria	I can . . . • Speak with the full faculty about the importance of coaching and how it will impact student learning • Create choice, ownership, and autonomy for how teachers engage in coaching cycles • Celebrate teachers who are engaging and learning from coaching cycles • Work with the coach to develop systems and resources for engaging teachers in coaching cycles		

Understand Pedagogy and Curriculum Content

	Accomplished	Developing	Novice
The School Leader	Expectations for instructional practice are clearly set and defined. Practices are aligned with the school improvement plan. The coach's role is to provide support so that teachers can meet this expectation.	Expectations for the instructional practice are clearly set and defined. Practices are aligned with the school improvement plan. The coach's role is to provide support so that teachers can meet this expectation.	The school leader takes a hands-off approach to leading instruction, allows the teachers to make decisions, and lays little groundwork regarding what is expected.
	The school leader has a well-developed pedagogical understanding and is able to recognize and provide feedback to teachers in direct relationship to the expected teaching practices.	The school leader has a developing sense of pedagogy and may understand some areas of instruction better than others. The school leader is able to provide specific feedback in some areas but not all.	The school leader lacks pedagogical understanding and is therefore unable to provide teachers with specific expectations and feedback regarding instruction.
	The school leader understands the curriculum and what it means for students.	The school leader understands some of, but not all, the curriculum that is used in the school.	The school leader does not understand the curriculum that is used in the school.

Understand Pedagogy and Curriculum Content			
	Accomplished	**Developing**	**Novice**
Success Criteria	I can . . . • Recognize effective instructional practice across subjects and content areas • Spend time in classrooms to look for the use of effective instructional practice • Work in partnership with the coach in service to teaching and learning • Set the expectation that teachers are implementing effective instructional practice as well as the curriculum • Learn and grow my understanding of effective instructional practice • Learn and grow my understanding of the content and curriculum		

Separate Coaching From Supervision			
	Accomplished	**Developing**	**Novice**
The School Leader	The school leader never asks the coach to engage in coaching that feels evaluative to teachers (i.e., walk-throughs, observations with checklists). The school leader uses coaching conversations to differentiate supervision practices. The school leader uses differentiated supervision practices to get the pulse of the school.	The school leader may ask the coach to engage in coaching that feels evaluative to teachers (i.e., walk-throughs, observations with checklists). Coaching conversations sometimes lead to evaluation. The school leader uses one to two supervision practices infrequently and has a limited knowledge of the pulse of the school.	The school leader expects the coach to hold teachers accountable. This involves more evaluative coaching (i.e., walk-throughs, observations with checklists). The school leader uses coaching conversations to identify teachers who need to be on formal evaluation plans. The school leader relies heavily on one supervision practice and has a limited knowledge of the pulse of the school.
Success Criteria	I can . . . • Support the coach to build trusting relationships with teachers • Build trusting relationships as the school principal • Avoid assigning coaching to people on improvement plans • Use differentiated supervision practices • Separate the coach from evaluative duties (i.e., walk-throughs, observations with checklists). Continue to learn and grow my understanding of effective instructional practices • Continue to learn and grow my understanding of the content and curriculum		

Support the Coach to Develop as a Practitioner			
	Accomplished	**Developing**	**Novice**
The School Leader	The school or district leader understands and supports the implementation of student-centered coaching. Time is allocated for the coach and principal to meet on a regular basis. The coach receives feedback regarding how coaching is going. Evaluation of coaching is aligned with the core practices for student-centered coaching.	The school or district is developing an understanding of student-centered coaching. The principal and coach meet informally to touch base, and support for the coach is less predictable and consistent. Evaluation of coaching is generic and doesn't identify student-centered coaching practices.	The school or district is developing an understanding of student-centered coaching. The principal and coach do not meet together or work collaboratively. Evaluation of coaching is not aligned with the core practices for student-centered coaching.
Success Criteria	I can . . . • Meet with the coach on a regular basis (weekly or biweekly) and ask open-ended questions about his or her coaching work • Create conditions where the coach feels comfortable taking a learning stance • Evaluate the impact of the coaching program with an aligned framework • Observe the coach on a regular basis • Provide strengths-based feedback to the coach • Evaluate the coach using the Rubric for Student-Centered Coaching		

Appendix B

Rubric for Student-Centered Coaching

Effective Coaches:

1. Understand and implement the core practices for student-centered coaching

2. Design systems and structures to engage teachers in coaching cycles

3. Understand effective instruction and help teachers implement it

4. Build trusting and respectful relationships with teachers

5. Provide skilled facilitation during collaboration and professional learning

6. Maintain a learning stance

7. Engage in reflective dialogue with teachers

Understand and Implement the Core Practices for Student-Centered Coaching			
	Accomplished	Developing	Novice
The Coach	The coach consistently implements the core practices for student-centered coaching. Thus, coaching leads to a measurable impact on instructional practice and student learning. The core practices are being implemented throughout the school community.	The coach is developing skill and confidence in using the core practices for student-centered coaching. The core practices are being used with some teachers but not the full school community.	The coach is using practices for coaching that aren't student-centered. This may include providing resources, holding teachers accountable for implementing programs, or serving as a quasi-administrator.

(Continued)

(Continued)

Understand and Implement the Core Practices for Student-Centered Coaching			
	Accomplished	**Developing**	**Novice**
Success Criteria	I can . . . • Organize most of my work to take place in coaching cycles • Work with teachers to set standards-based goals for coaching cycles • Work with teachers to unpack the goal into student-friendly learning targets • Use student evidence when co-planning and co-teaching • Co-plan lessons that integrate effective instructional practices • Use co-teaching practices that build partnerships with teachers • Measure the impact of coaching cycles on student and teacher learning		

Design Systems and Structures to Engage Teachers in Coaching Cycles			
	Accomplished	**Developing**	**Novice**
The Coach	The coach creates a well-organized system for managing coaching cycles that provides choice for how teachers can engage.	The coach offers some coaching cycles, but there is limited reach and/or effectiveness. Teachers aren't sure how or why they should engage in coaching cycles.	The coach spends very little time in coaching cycles and mostly serves as a resource to teachers.
Success Criteria	I can . . . • Set agreements with teachers before the coaching cycle begins • Ensure that teachers have choice and ownership throughout a coaching cycle • Maintain focus on the goal that was set by the teacher • Provide opportunities to engage in coaching cycles throughout the school year • Use logs and note taking in a way that is transparent and includes the teacher • Continually listen and respond to the needs of teachers • Design and use a system for monitoring teacher participation in coaching cycles to engage others		

Understand Effective Instruction and Help Teachers Implement It			
	Accomplished	**Developing**	**Novice**
The Coach	The coach has an extensive understanding of effective instructional practices across grades and subjects. The coach successfully supports others to implement these practices in their own classrooms.	The coach has some understanding of effective instructional practices but is learning how to transfer knowledge to the work of other teachers.	The coach either doesn't have a fully developed understanding of effective instructional practices and/or is unable to move teachers toward their own implementation.

Understand Effective Instruction and Help Teachers Implement It			
	Accomplished	**Developing**	**Novice**
Success Criteria	I can . . . • Articulate what effective practices are and why they matter to student learning • Prioritize which practices to focus on at any given time • Help move teachers forward in their learning while maintaining their ownership of the process • Use student evidence when co-planning with teachers • Co-plan with teachers in a way that intentionally builds effective practices into lessons • Co-teach to implement effective instructional practice • Continue to learn and grow in using effective instructional practices		

Build Trusting and Respectful Relationships With Teachers			
	Accomplished	**Developing**	**Novice**
The Coach	The coach works effectively with all teachers because of specific measures he or she has taken to build trusting and professional relationships.	The coach is beginning to build trusting relationships with a broader array of teachers, including more challenging teachers.	The coach is able to build trusting relationships with a limited group of teachers.
Success Criteria	I can . . . • Build collegial relationships that are trusting and respectful • Use a respectful tone throughout my coaching conversations • Avoid being a "teller," but rather a "co-constructor" of learning • Avoid focusing on weaknesses, but rather build on strengths • Ask open-ended questions • Set a tone that "we are all learners"		

Provide Skilled Facilitation During Collaboration			
	Accomplished	**Developing**	**Novice**
The Coach	The coach understands which facilitation processes to employ at any given time. The coach is a skilled facilitator and, as a result, both small and large groups function in a highly productive manner on a consistent basis.	The coach is working to expand the repertoire of facilitation techniques used in small and large group sessions. Groups are beginning to function at a more productive level.	The coach employs a limited set of facilitation processes. Small and/or large group facilitation are not productive on a consistent basis.

(Continued)

(Continued)

Provide Skilled Facilitation During Collaboration			
	Accomplished	**Developing**	**Novice**
Success Criteria	I can . . . <ul><li>Use strategies for facilitation to guide group learning</li><li>Use (or create) protocols that contribute to the learning of the group</li><li>Anchor conversations in student work</li><li>Encourage teacher choice and ownership during collaboration</li><li>Listen and respond in a way that honors the group</li><li>Use the Seven Norms of Collaborative Work to support teachers to reflect as learners</li><li>Manage interactions between peers in a collegial way</li><li>Respectfully intervene if collegial interactions are toxic or harmful</li></ul>		

Maintain a Learning Stance			
	Accomplished	**Developing**	**Novice**
The Coach	The coach consistently seeks new experiences and opportunities for learning rather than taking the stance of an "expert."	The coach takes advantage of some opportunities for new learning and is becoming more comfortable regarding taking the stance of "co-learner" with teachers.	The coach does not take advantage of opportunities for new learning on a consistent basis and does not take the stance of "co-learner" with teachers.
Success Criteria	I can . . . <ul><li>Demonstrate that I am a learner inside and outside of school</li><li>Take risks that are inherent to learning</li><li>Share how my thinking evolves based on the input of others</li><li>Build collegial relationships based on my own learning</li><li>Establish a trusting and respectful tone throughout my coaching conversations</li><li>Create systems for teachers to share ideas and resources with one another</li></ul>		

Engage in Reflective Dialogue With Teachers			
	Accomplished	**Developing**	**Novice**
The Coach	The coach encourages reflective dialogue by asking open-ended questions, probing, and using paraphrasing techniques rather than simply giving the teacher answers.	The coach is beginning to use strategies such as asking open-ended questions, probing, and paraphrasing techniques to encourage reflective dialogue among teachers.	The coach does not use conversational approaches that encourage reflective dialogue among teachers.

Engage in Reflective Dialogue With Teachers			
	Accomplished	**Developing**	**Novice**
Success Criteria	I can . . . • Use student work as a means of encouraging reflection • Listen (avoid talking too much or making too many suggestions that may overwhelm teachers) • Take a strengths-based approach to conversations • Paraphrase to honor and/or clarify the thoughts of others • Ask probing questions that I don't know the answer to • Maintain an open mind as the teachers' learning progresses		

Appendix C

Sample School Improvement Plan

SCHOOL IMPROVEMENT AND PROFESSIONAL DEVELOPMENT PLAN EXAMPLE

Overview

School Improvement Team Members

Principal Advisory Team: (Tracy F., Penny G., Lyndsey S., Amy T., Brenda P., Liz S.)

Math Team: (Kevin M., Sue H., Jane W., Elizabeth B.)

Literacy Team: (Bev J., Nanci J., Jean C., Stephanie K., Jason H., Danielle A., Mary Jane A.)

The primary goal for school improvement is to monitor student learning toward mastering grade level expectations and learning targets daily, weekly, and monthly with formative assessments and then respond with appropriate individual, small group, and/or whole group instruction.

The principal prepared an assessment portfolio and participated in a data consult with the District's Executive Director of Curriculum and Instruction. Data prepared for the consult were shared with various team members as well as with a parent committee. During the last 2 weeks of school, team members reviewed the data and participated in articulating school improvement goals and strategies.

SUMMARY OF GOALS AND STRATEGIES

Goal Areas	Goal	Strategy
Literacy	By May of 2016, 78% of the students will perform at proficient levels in reading as measured by our literacy assessment wall and will grow at least +14 standard scale points on the state assessments.	Use learning targets and success criteria to respond to monitor and respond to student needs.
Math	By May of 2016, 72% of the students will perform at proficient levels in mathematics as measured by our math assessment wall and will grow at least +14 standard scale points on the state assessments.	Same as above
Safe and Respectful School	By May of 2016, 75% of the students will perform at proficient or advanced as measured by our behavior data wall.	Implement instructional discipline process

ACADEMIC GOALS

A1-Literacy Goal: By May of 2016, 78% of the students will perform at proficient levels in reading as measured by our literacy assessment wall and will grow at least +14 standard scale points on the state assessments.

A2-Math Goal: By May of 2016, 72% of the students will perform at proficient levels in mathematics as measured by our math assessment wall and will grow at least +14 standard scale points on the state assessments.

STRATEGY

Strategy	Use learning targets and success criteria to respond to monitor and respond to student needs
Evidence of Strategy Implementation:	

Observational Data:

- Walk-throughs and formal observations with focused feedback on monitoring and responding
- Professional development (PD) and professional learning community (PLC) agendas that are focused on analyzing and responding

Collected Evidence:

- Teacher-created tools to monitor progress and to collect data toward learning targets
- Shared action steps to respond to common, formative assessment results
- Gap analysis on Tier 1 literacy intervention results
- Data dig results that identify mastered and non-mastered learning targets
- Formative assessments that are created in PLCs and analyzed

ACTION STEPS

KEY: *I = Initiate, P = Progressing, M = Met, C = Canceled*

Action Steps #	Action Steps to Implement Strategy	Person Responsible	I	P	M	C
A1	Define and share PLC learning cycle	Principal, PLC leaders	June			
A2	Learn about learning targets and success criteria	Principal, Coach	Sept			
A3	Develop learning targets and success criteria	All	All year			
A4	Create performances of understanding	Principal, PLCs	Nov			
A5	Monitor progress and collect formative data	Principal, PLCs	Nov–May			
A6	Learn how to respond when students are not meeting targets	Principals, Coaches, PLCs	Nov–May			

SAFE AND RESPECTFUL SCHOOLS GOAL

SRS Goal: By May of 2016, 75% of the students will perform at proficient or advanced as measured by our behavior data wall.

STRATEGY

Strategy	Implement Instructional Discipline
Evidence of Strategy Implementation:	

Observational Data:

- Walk-throughs and formal observations with focused feedback on students needing behavior intervention

Collected Evidence:

- Articulation of behavior interventions
- Progress monitoring of implemented behavior interventions
- Office referrals
- District climate survey
- Behavior data wall data

ACTION STEPS

KEY: *I = Initiate, P = Progressing, M = Met, C = Canceled*

Action Steps #	Action Steps to Implement Strategy	Person Responsible	I	P	M	C
A1	Implement a Determining Appropriate Intervention Services (DAIS) behavior team	Principal, PLC leaders	June			
A2	Articulate our driving pillars of behavior (i.e., respect, responsibility, etc.)	All	Aug			
A3	Study and implement framework of instructional discipline (instruction, prevention, reinforcement, logical consequences)	Teachers, Principal, School Psychologist, Behavior Specialist	Sept			
A4	Implement collaborative problem solving	Teachers, Principal, School Psychologist, Behavior Specialist	All year			
A5	Monitor progress	Principal, PLCs	Sept– May			

Professional Development Preservice days will include updating staff on school improvement plans and setting building expectations for behavior.

Early Release Focus (weekly)	*PLC Focus	Date
Whole Group: Collaborative problem solving approach Small Group: Identifying common classroom procedures by grade level	Goal setting	Sept. 15
Whole Group: Learning Targets and Success Criteria Small Group (PLC): Literacy learning targets	Math	Sept. 30
Whole Group: Learning Targets and Success Criteria Small Group: Literacy learning targets	Math	Oct. 7
Whole Group: Evidence of Learning Small Group: Literacy evidence of student learning	Math	Oct. 14
Whole Group: Evidence of Learning Small Group: Data wall	Math	Oct. 21
Whole Group: Reviewing Plan Bs (instructional discipline) Small Group: Behavior data wall	Literacy	Oct. 28
Whole Group: Using descriptors Small Group: Math learning targets	Literacy	Nov. 4
Whole Group: Using descriptors Small Group: Math learning targets	Literacy	Nov. 11
Whole Group: Monitoring learning Small Group: Math evidence of learning	Literacy	Nov. 18
Whole Group: Monitoring learning Small Group: Literacy	Math	Nov. 25
Whole Group: Feedback that feeds forward Small Group: Literacy	Math	Dec. 2
Whole Group: Feedback that feeds forward Small Group: Literacy	Math	Dec. 9

(Continued)

(Continued)

Early Release Focus (weekly)	*PLC Focus	Date
Whole Group: Celebration checkpoint Small Group: Data wall	Math	Dec. 16
Whole Group: Strategies for Plan B students Small Group: Behavior interventions	Literacy	Jan. 6
Whole Group: Feedback that feeds forward Small Group: Math	Literacy	Jan. 13
Whole Group: Responding when kids don't learn Small Group: Math	Literacy	Jan. 20
Whole Group: District PD	Literacy	Jan. 27
Whole Group: Responding when kids don't learn Small Group: Data wall	Math	Feb. 3
Whole Group: Responding when kids don't learn Small Group: Reading	Math	Feb. 10
Whole Group: Responding when kids don't learn Small Group: Reading	Math	Feb. 17
Whole Group: Shared meaning of strategies when students miss learning targets Small Group: Reading	Math	Feb. 24
Whole Group: Shared meaning of strategies when students miss learning targets Small Group: Math	Literacy	March 3
Whole Group: Shared meaning of strategies when students miss learning targets Small Group: Math	Literacy	March 10
Whole Group: Checking in on instructional discipline Small Group: Math	Literacy	March 17

Early Release Focus (weekly)	*PLC Focus	Date
Whole Group: Checking in on instructional discipline Small Group: Math	Literacy	March 24
Whole Group: Monitoring Update, where are we, what do we need? Small Group: Reading	Math	April 7
Whole Group: Learning Targets, what is working? Small Group: Reading	Math	April 14
Whole Group: Success Criteria, what is working? Small Group: Reading	Math	April 21
Whole Group: Performance of understanding, what is working? Small Group: Reading	Math	April 28
Whole Group: Descriptors, what is working? Small Group: Math	Literacy	May 5
Whole Group: Evidence of learning what is working Small Group: Math	Literacy	May 12
Whole Group: Reflection and planning for next year Small Group: Reading	Math	May 24
Whole Group: Goal setting	Celebration	June 2

*Indicates the content focus for PLC time; the PLC learning cycle will be the process used.

Appendix D

Student-Centered Coaching Moves

SETTING GOALS FOR COACHING CYCLES

Coaches:

- Use the standards to drive goal-setting conversations.
- If possible, align the goal with a unit of study.
- If possible, use relevant data to drive the goal-setting conversation.
- Ask open-ended questions when setting goals with teachers.
- Avoid goals that emphasize only skills, aim for complex learning.
- Confirm that the teacher values the goal that was set for the coaching cycle.
- Avoid setting goals for pockets of students, try to set them for the whole class.
- Use a coaching log to stay focused and organized.

USING LEARNING TARGETS

Coaches:

- Work with the teacher(s) to unpack the coaching cycle goal into learning targets.
- Make sure the learning targets are student friendly and clear.
- Aim for a balance of knowledge and skills when creating learning targets.
- Ask open-ended questions so the teacher reflects on where he or she wants the students to be as a result of the coaching cycle.
- Use a coaching log to stay focused and organized.

CO-PLANNING SESSIONS

Coaches:

- Sort student evidence with the teacher in a collaborative manner.
- Use student evidence to determine instructional next steps.
- Plan how you will co-teach the next lesson with the teacher.
- Ask open-ended questions so the teacher is in the driver's seat.
- Paraphrase so the teacher knows you've been listening.
- Use a coaching log to stay focused and organized.

CO-TEACHING LESSONS

Coaches:

- Collect evidence while in the classroom.
- Use learning targets as the guide for collecting student evidence.
- Share the evidence that is collected with the teacher.
- Encourage the teacher to collect student evidence using the same process.
- Be specific and descriptive in the evidence that is collected.
- Use a tool, such as a student grid, to collect evidence.
- Set norms with the teacher before co-teaching.
- Provide options for co-teaching (noticing and naming, thinking aloud, teaching in tandem, you pick four, and micro modeling).
- Only co-teach lessons that have been co-planned (avoid popping in).
- Guide the teacher to address students' needs based on the evidence that is collected.

PROVIDE STRENGTHS-BASED FEEDBACK

Coaches:

- Ask clarifying questions before providing feedback.
- Observe instruction or analyze student evidence to get a clearer picture.
- Value the teacher by celebrating growth.
- Uncover possibilities through co-planning next steps.
- Ask open-ended questions.
- Keep an open mind and honor the teacher as a learner.

MEASURING THE IMPACT OF STUDENT-CENTERED COACHING

Coaches:

- Engage in coaching cycles to take coaching deeper.
- Use the Results-Based Coaching Tool (See Appendix E) to measure teacher and student growth across a coaching cycle.
- Capture data at the beginning and end of the coaching cycle with a pre-assessment.
- Co-teach between one and three times per week.
- Co-plan at least once a week.
- Engage in a reflective conversation, or exit interview, at the end of the coaching cycle to learn how the coaching benefited the teacher and students.
- Reflect on how to improve the coaching based on the feedback that is provided.

FACILITATING STUDENT-CENTERED LEARNING LABS

Coaches:

- Use student-centered learning labs as a job-embedded method of professional learning.
- Organize learning labs to occur a few times across the school year.
- Support the teacher who will be hosting observers through a coaching cycle that occurs in advance of the learning lab.
- Set norms.
- Facilitate the learning lab, including the prebrief, the observation, and debrief.
- Plan the learning lab, get the necessary coverage, and help teachers understand the purpose for this type of professional learning.

ENGAGING IN RIGOROUS DISCOURSE

Coaches:

- Use techniques such as paraphrasing, listening, and asking open-ended questions.
- Refrain from passing judgement.

(Continued)

(Continued)

- Understand that learning is a progression and that teacher development takes time.
- Take notes in a way that doesn't take away from the conversation.
- Put one or two ideas on the table, don't overwhelm the teacher with too many ideas.

Appendix E

Results-Based Coaching Tool

Results-Based Coaching Tool

Teacher:			Coach:	
Coaching Cycle Focus:			**Dates of Coaching Cycle:**	

Standards-Based Goal What is the goal for student learning?	**Focus for Teacher Learning** What instructional practices will help students reach the goal?	**Student-Centered Coaching** What coaching practices were implemented during this coaching cycle?	**Teacher Learning** As a result of the coaching cycle, what instructional practices are being used on a consistent basis?	**Student Learning** How did student achievement increase as a result of the coaching cycle?
Students will . . . *Standard(s):* *Learning Targets:* I can: *Baseline Data:* _____ Emerging _____ Developing _____ Meeting _____ Exceeding _____ % of students were able to demonstrate proficiency of the learning targets.	**Teacher will . . .**	**Coach and Teacher did . . .** (check those that apply) ☐ Goal setting ☐ Creating learning targets ☐ Analysis of student work ☐ Co-teaching ☐ Collecting student evidence during the class period ☐ Collaborative planning ☐ Shared learning to build knowledge of content and pedagogy	**Teacher is . . .**	**Students are . . .** *Post-Assessment Data:* _____ Emerging _____ Developing _____ Meeting _____ Exceeding _____ % of students were able to demonstrate proficiency of the learning targets. *Follow up for students who didn't reach the goal:*

REFLECTION QUESTIONS FOR THE RESULTS-BASED COACHING TOOL

Teacher Reflections	Coach Reflections
What worked well for you during our collaboration and coaching cycle? How has your teaching been positively impacted?	What worked well for you during our collaboration and coaching cycle?
How do you feel our collaboration has positively impacted the students?	How do you feel our collaboration positively impacted the students?
What were any challenges or missed opportunities during our work together?	What were any challenges or missed opportunities during our work together?
What are some next steps in your teaching?	What are some next steps in your coaching?

Appendix F

Planner for Sharing Lessons

Learning Target(s):

Lesson Components	What It Will Look Like	Who Will Take the Lead? What Will the Other "Teacher" Do?

Source: Sweeney, D., & Harris, L. (2016). *Student-Centered Coaching: The Moves*. Thousand Oaks, CA: Corwin. Used with permission.

FOURTH GRADE MATHEMATICS LESSON WITH HEATHER AND ROBYN

Learning Target: *I can solve two-digit multiplication problems using the most efficient strategy.*

Lesson Components	What It Will Look Like	Who Will Take the Lead? What Will the Other "Teacher" Do?
Formative Assessment	Students will solve the following problem to assess the strategies they are using when they encounter two-digit multiplication. Problem is: 57 x 33. The students will solve the problem on half sheets so that the coach and teacher can quickly sort them before the reteach.	Robyn will get the students started with the problem. Then they will collect and sort the student evidence.
Guided Practice	Students solve more problems that are determined based on how they did with the formative assessment. This time they will work on whiteboards. Showing how they solved the problem will be emphasized. An anchor chart will be used to capture the different methods that the students are using.	Heather will *micro model* how she assesses problem-solving strategies. Robyn and Heather will monitor student learning and check in with each other to determine how to scaffold students' learning.
Share	Students share how they went about solving the problems. As they share, they will be asked if this is the most efficient strategy and if they got the correct answer.	Heather and Robyn will teach this in tandem.

Source: Sweeney, D., & Harris, L. (2016). *Student-Centered Coaching: The Moves.* Thousand Oaks, CA: Corwin. Used with permission.

EIGHTH GRADE READING WITH JAMES AND LISA

Learning Target: *I can analyze how the form or structure of a text contributes to its meaning and style.*

Lesson Components	What It Will Look Like	Who Will Take the Lead? What Will the Other "Teacher" Do?
Reflect on the Learning Target	Students will reflect on the learning target with a partner. *Learning Target: I can analyze how the form or structure of a text contributes to its meaning and style.*	Lisa *micro models* this part of the lesson. James has set this as a goal for his teaching and would like Lisa to demonstrate what it looks like to have students self-assess against a learning target. As Lisa *micro models,* she will *think aloud* so that James gets a sense of what she is thinking throughout this portion of the lesson.
Mini Lesson	In the lesson, James will remind the students of the following elements of fiction: plot, character, setting, and conflict. This will be review. Then he will use examples of familiar literature to illustrate how fiction writers create structure around these elements. James will *think aloud* using a book that he is currently reading where each chapter is written in the voice of a different character. He will explain how this lends itself to a character-based plot structure. Last, he will *think aloud* about how the structure supports the overall meaning of the book.	James teaches the mini lesson. He requested for Lisa to clarify and add on if she notices any confusion. She may also redirect any students who aren't engaged.
Discussion Groups	Students work in small groups to discuss the texts they are reading. Their prompt: *Which is the most dominant feature of your book: plot, character, setting, or conflict? How does this contribute to the overall meaning of the book?*	Lisa and James work with small groups. Their plan is to stick together so they can hear the same conversations. This way they will be able to take what they hear into account when they co-plan.
Reflect	After the small groups, the students reflect on the learning target one more time. This is done on an index card and is turned in at the end of the class period.	Lisa and James collect student evidence by listening to what the students say and how they explain their thinking. They also review the index cards during their co-planning session.

Source: Sweeney, D., & Harris, L. (2016). *Student-Centered Coaching: The Moves.* Thousand Oaks, CA: Corwin. Used with permission.

References

Amabile, T., & Kramer, S. (2011). *The progress principle: Using small wins to ignite joy, engagement, and creativity at work*. Boston, MA: Harvard Business Review Press.

Bambrick-Santoya, P. (2010). *Driven by data: A practical guide to improve instruction*. San Francisco, CA: Jossey-Bass.

Bandura, A. (1997). *Self-efficacy: The exercise of control*. New York, NY: W. H. Freeman.

Bansford, J. D., Brown, A. L., & Cocking, R. R. (Eds.). (2000). *How people learn: Brain, mind, experience, and school*. Washington, DC: National Academy Press.

Bloomberg, P., & Pitchford, B. (2017). *Leading impact teams: Building a culture of efficacy*. Thousand Oaks, CA: Corwin.

Booher, D. (1992). *Executive's portfolio of model speeches for all occasions*. Upper Saddle River, NJ: Prentice Hall.

Brown, B. (2012). *Daring greatly: How the courage to be vulnerable transforms the way we live, love, parent, and lead*. New York, NY: Penguin Random House.

Bryk, A. S., & Schneider, B. L. (2002). *Trust in schools: A core resource for improvement*. New York, NY: Russell Sage Foundation.

Burch, G. (1970). "Conscious competence learning model matrix: Four stages of learning theory – unconscious incompetence to unconscious competence matrix – and other theories and models for learning and change." Retrieved from https://www.businessballs.com/self-awareness/conscious-competence-learning-model-63/

Campitelli, G., & Gobet, F. (2011). Deliberate practice: Necessary but not sufficient. *Current Directions in Psychological Science, 20*(5), 280–285.

Cheliotes, L., & Reilly, M. (2010). *Coaching conversations: Transforming your school one conversation at a time*. Thousand Oaks, CA: Corwin.

Danielson, C. (2016). Charlotte Danielson on rethinking teacher evaluation. *Education Week, 35*(28), 20–24.

Danielson, C., & McGreal, T. (2000). *Teacher evaluation: To enhance professional practice*. Alexandria, VA: ASCD.

Donohoo, J. (2017). *Collective efficacy: How educators' beliefs impact student learning*. Thousand Oaks, CA: Corwin.

DuFour, R., Eaker, R., & DuFour, R. (2005). *On common ground: The power of professional learning communities*. Bloomington, IN: National Educational Service.

Dweck, C. (2006). *Mindset: The new psychology of success*. New York, NY: Ballantine Books.

Elmore, R. F. (2004). *School reform from the inside out*. Cambridge, MA: Harvard Education Press.

Elmore, R. F. (2008). Leadership as the practice of improvement. In B. Pont, D. Nusche, & D. Hopkins (Eds.). *Improving school leadership volume 2: Case studies on system leadership* (2nd ed., pp. 21–25). Paris, France: Organisation for Economic Co-Operation and Development.

Flaherty, J. (1999). *Coaching: Evoking excellence in others*. Boston, MA: Butterworth-Heinemann.

Fullan, M. (2009). *Motion leadership: The skinny on becoming change savvy*. Thousand Oaks, CA: Corwin.

Fullan, M. (2014). *The principal: Three keys to maximizing impact*. San Francisco, CA: Jossey-Bass.

Fullan, M., & Quinn, J. (2016). *Coherence: The right drivers in action for schools, districts, and systems*. Thousand Oaks, CA: Corwin.

Goodwin, B. (2013). Research says/Teacher leadership: No guarantee of success. *Educational Leadership, 71*(2), 78–80.

Gorski, P. (2008). The myth of the culture of poverty. *Educational Leadership, 65*(7), 32–36.

Guskey, T. (2002). Does it make a difference? Evaluating professional development. *Educational Leadership, 59*(6), 45–51.

Hargreaves, A., & Fullan, M. (2012). *Professional capital: Transforming teaching in every school*. New York, NY: Teachers College Press & Toronto, ON: Ontario Principals Council.

Hattie, J. (2015). *What works best in education: The politics of collective expertise*. London, UK: Pearson.

Heffernan, M. (2015). *Beyond measure: The big impact of small changes*. New York, NY: Simon & Schuster.

Heineke, S., & Polnick, B. (2013). Pave the way for coaches: Principal's actions are key to shaping roles and relationships. *Learning Forward, 34*(3), 48–51.

Joyce, B., & Showers, B. (1980). Improving inservice training: The messages of research. *Educational Leadership, 37*(5), 379–385.

Killion, J., Harrison, C., Bryan, C., & Clifton, H. (2012). *Coaching matters*. Oxford, OH: Learning Forward.

Kirtman, L., & Fullan, M. (2016). *Leadership: Key competencies for whole-system change*. Bloomington, IN: Solution Tree Press.

Kluger, J. (2009). *Simplexity: Why simple things become complex (and how complex things can become simple)*. New York, NY: Hyperion Books.

Kraft, M., Blazar, D., & Hogan, D. (2016). *The effect of teacher coaching on instruction and achievement: A meta-analysis of the causal evidence*. Brown University Working Paper.

Leithwood, K., Day, C., Sammons, P., Harris, A., & Hopkins, D. (2006). *Seven strong claims about successful school leadership*. Nottingham, UK: National College for School Leadership/Department of Education and Skills.

Lemov, D. (2010). *Teach like a champion: 49 techniques that put students on the path to college*. San Francisco, CA: Jossey-Bass.

Marshall, K. (2013). *Rethinking teacher supervision and evaluation: How to work smart, build collaboration, and close the achievement gap* (2nd ed.). San Francisco, CA: Jossey-Bass.

Mausbach, A., & Morrison, K. (2016). *School leadership through the seasons: A guide to staying focused and getting results all year*. New York, NY: Routledge.

Mooney N. J., & Mausbach, A. T. (2008). *Align the design: A blueprint for school improvement*. Alexandria, VA: ASCD.

Moss, C., Brookhart, S., & Long, B. (2011). Knowing your learning target. *Educational Leadership, 68*(6), 66–69.

Murray, S., Ma, X., & Mazur, J. (2009). Effects of peer coaching on teachers' collaborative interactions and students' mathematics achievement. *Journal of Educational Research. 103*(2), 203–212.

Pink, D. (2009). *Drive: The surprising truth about what motivates us*. New York, NY: Riverhead Books.

Robinson, V. (2011). *Student-centered leadership*. Hoboken, NJ: Jossey-Bass.

Robinson, V. (2018). *Reduce chance to increase improvement*. Thousand Oaks, CA: Corwin.

Rostron, S. S. (2009). *Business coaching international: Transforming individuals and organizations*. London, UK: Karnac Books.

Schmoker, M. (2011). First things first: Curriculum now. *Phi Delta Kappan, 93*(3), 70–71.

Senge, P. (2006). *The fifth discipline: The art and practice of the learning organization*. New York, NY: Doubleday.

Sinek, S. (2009). *Start with why: How great leaders inspire everyone to take action*. New York, NY: Penguin Books.

Sinek, S. (2015). Lecture: Leaders eat last: Why some teams come together and others don't [Video]. Retrieved from http://www.sai-iowa.org/leaders-eat-last-book-study.cfm

Sweeney, D. (2003). *Learning along the way*. Portland, ME: Stenhouse.

Sweeney, D. (2011). *Student-centered coaching: A guide for K–8 principals and coaches*. Thousand Oaks, CA: Corwin.

Sweeney, D. (2013). *Student-centered coaching at the secondary level*. Thousand Oaks, CA: Corwin.

Sweeney, D., & Harris, L. (2016). *Student-centered coaching: The moves*. Thousand Oaks, CA: Corwin.

Tomlinson, C. A. (2014). The bridge between today's lesson and tomorrow's. *Educational Leadership, 71*(6), 10–14.

Tschannen-Moran, M., & Hoy, W. K. (2000). A multidisciplinary analysis of the nature, meaning, and measurement of trust. *Review of Educational Research, 70*(4), 547–593,

Van De Walle, J. A., Karp, K. S., Bay-Williams, J. M. (2012). *Elementary and middle school mathematics: Teaching developmentally*. New York, NY: Pearson.

Vela, J. (2002). *Learning to listen, learning to teach: The power of dialogue in educating adults*. San Francisco, CA: Jossey-Bass.

Wiggins, G., & McTighe, J. (2005). *Understanding by design*. Alexandria, VA: ASCD.

Wiking, M. (2014). The happy Danes: Exploring the reasons behind the high levels of happiness in Denmark. Retrieved from https://docs.wixstatic.com/ugd/928487_7f341890e9484a279416ffbc9dc95ff4.pdf

Index

A SAGE Publishing Company

Helping educators make the greatest impact

CORWIN HAS ONE MISSION: to enhance education through intentional professional learning.

We build long-term relationships with our authors, educators, clients, and associations who partner with us to develop and continuously improve the best evidence-based practices that establish and support lifelong learning.

Solutions you want. Experts you trust. Results you need.